The Bible from Scratch

The Bible. It's a big book. As big as life itself. Between its covers are shipwrecks, plagues of locusts, loves won and lost, feuding brothers, Sodom and Gomorrah, fiery prophets, visions of the future, awesome encounters with God, and water turned into wine. To name but a few.

No surprise that it's been the world's best-seller since the year dot.

But surely it's too heavy for *me* to understand?

If you find the Bible a bit difficult, a bit too formidable to break into, then *The Bible from Scratch* could be for you.

It gives a lightning sketch of the Bible using easy-to-digest graphics. It explains the meaning of every book (including Habakkuk). It introduces all the famous faces, events, miracles, etc.

Simon Jenkins is an author, editor, illustrator and part-time human being. A graduate in theology, he was once a London bus conductor and editor of the satirical magazine *Ship of Fools*. He now lives in London with his wife and two children. He is also author of Lion's *Bible Mapbook*.

Copyright © 1987 Simon Jenkins

Published by
Lion Publishing plc
Icknield Way, Tring, Herts, England
ISBN 0 7459 1004 1
Lion Publishing Corporation
1705 Hubbard Avenue, Batavia, Illinois 60510, USA
ISBN 0 7459 1004 1
Albatross Books Pty Ltd
PO Box 320, Sutherland, NSW 2232, Australia
ISBN 0 86760 880 3

First edition 1987

Quotations from *Good News Bible*, copyright 1966,
1971 and 1976 American Bible Society; published
by Bible Societies/Collins

Quotations from *New International Version*:
copyright © New York International Bible Society,
1978

British Library Cataloguing in Publication Data
Jenkins, Simon
    The Bible from Scratch.
    1. Bible—Criticism, interpretation, etc.
    I. Title
    220.6   BS511.2
    ISBN 0-7459-1004-1

Library of Congress Cataloging in Publication Data
Jenkins, Simon
    The Bible from Scratch.
    I. Bible—Introductions.   I. Title.
    BS475.2.J46   1987   220.6'1   86-27491
    ISBN 0-7459-1004-1

Printed and bound in Great Britain by
Cox & Wyman Ltd, Reading

THE BIBLE FROM SCRATCH

S I M O N   J E N K I N S

A LION BOOK
Tring · Batavia · Sydney

For Talitha +
Nathan

May you find it
a Book too big
to grow out of...

INTRODUCTION

What's this? The Bible explained in cartoons? Whatever would Moses say? Or Habakkuk? Would Elijah have burned it? And would Paul turn in his catacomb to see his life's work reduced to a few scribbles?

Probably not! Because the Bible's characters themselves were not shy about using different methods to communicate what they had to say. Jeremiah smashed crockery. Ezekiel performed some weird one-act plays. David sang songs. Nathan told a trick story. Paul wrote letters. Jesus talked in pictures.

And this drive to popularize has sometimes surfaced in the history of the church. St Augustine, heavyweight theologian though he was, used pop songs to attack the heretics. And John Calvin (no less) wrote Christian lyrics to Genevan jigs.

This book is offered in the same spirit. It's not a commentary or a complete introduction to each part of the Bible. But it is intended to give a genuine feel for what the Bible is about. To conjure up the sights, sounds, smells and tastes of the book. And it should help to orientate the reader who has suddenly parachuted into biblical territory.

I would like to say a special thank-you to my wife Roey for the time she gave up while this was being written, drawn, snipped and stuck together. Amazingly her patience only *increased* as we struggled through the tunnel towards the distant light of Revelation chapter 22.

The Bible is the world's best-selling book. But it's probably true to say that it's not the world's best-read book. If this book helps to make a dent in that statistic, it will have done its job.

Simon Jenkins

CONTENTS

THE OLD TESTAMENT

THE NEW TESTAMENT

THE BIBLE

PSSST!
BEFORE WE START...

JUST TO SAY THAT IN
THIS BOOK REFERENCES
TO BIBLE PASSAGES ARE
GIVEN IN THIS WAY:
2 KINGS 12:1-9.

2 KINGS MEANS IT'S
THE SECOND BOOK OF
KINGS. AND 12:1-9 MEANS
CHAPTER 12, VERSES 1
TO 9.

NOW READ ON...

WHAT IS THIS BOOK CALLED 'THE BIBLE'? PEOPLE SEE IT IN MANY DIFFERENT WAYS —

Ancient documents

A book of magical knowledge

That book on the shelf that we never read

The Jewish national archive

A big, forbidding book, full of 'Thou shalt nots'

The story of Jesus Christ, David, Paul, Moses, etc.

HOWEVER YOU COME TO THE BIBLE, IT'S WORTH STARTING TO READ IT FOR YOURSELF TO DISCOVER WHAT IT'S ALL ABOUT. BY ANY STANDARDS THE BIBLE IS ONE OF THE WORLD'S GREAT BOOKS (SOME SAY THE GREATEST) AND IT HAS A UNIQUE POWER TO CONVINCE PEOPLE WHO READ IT WITH AN OPEN MIND.

So what is it that makes the Bible different?

WELL, THE GOD DESCRIBED IN THE BIBLE ENJOYS LETTING PEOPLE KNOW ABOUT HIMSELF. THE TECHNICAL TERM FOR THIS IS 'REVELATION'.

GOD REVEALS HIMSELF THROUGH:

- ☐ THE WORLD AROUND US
- ☐ THE WAY WE ARE MADE
- ☐ THROUGH EXPERIENCE

AH-HAH!

THE BIBLE IS DIFFERENT FROM ANY OTHER BOOK BECAUSE IT CLAIMS TO BE NOTHING LESS THAN GOD REVEALING HIMSELF TO THE HUMAN RACE. THE BIBLE'S WRITERS WERE ON THE RECEIVING END OF GOD'S REVELATION. HERE'S HOW THEY PUT IT...

The Lord God said to me...

THE PROPHET JEREMIAH

I appeared to Abraham, to Isaac, and to Jacob as Almighty God...

GOD SPEAKS TO MOSES

I saw the Lord.

THE PROPHET ISAIAH

God revealed his secret plan and made it known to me.

THE APOSTLE PAUL

But how did it happen? Are you saying that the Bible was lowered from heaven on a rope, or something?

NO. THE BIBLE DIDN'T MAGICALLY APPEAR ONE DAY. INSTEAD, IT WAS WRITTEN OVER MANY CENTURIES BY DIFFERENT PEOPLE. IN THIS SENSE IT IS FULLY A HUMAN BOOK. THE DIFFERENCE IS THAT GOD CHOSE ITS WRITERS AND INSPIRED THEM TO WRITE IN SUCH A WAY THAT THEIR WORDS REVEALED THE CHARACTER AND THE PLANS OF GOD.

So God dictated the whole thing - like a boss to a secretary?

NO, NOT AT ALL. INSTEAD, GOD WAS INVOLVED IN THE WHOLE PROCESS OF WRITING, USING THE WRITERS' PERSONALITIES, CIRCUMSTANCES, WRITING STYLES AND TASTES TO COMMUNICATE WHAT HE HAD TO SAY. THIS INTIMATE RELATIONSHIP BETWEEN GOD AND THE WRITING OF THE BIBLE IS SUMMED UP IN THIS QUOTE —

"All Scripture is God-breathed..."
2 TIMOTHY 3:16

THIS MEANS THAT FOR CHRISTIANS THE BIBLE IS THE LAST WORD ON WHAT THEY BELIEVE AND HOW THEY SHOULD LIVE.

Mmm. Fascinating, I'm sure. But isn't it all rather serious, heavy and ....

Z Z Z Z Z Z

THE BIBLE IS A SERIOUS BOOK, BUT THAT DOESN'T MEAN IT'S A CURE FOR INSOMNIA. GOD SPEAKS TO US ON OUR TERMS— THROUGH THE EXPERIENCE OF WOMEN AND MEN. THIS MEANS THAT THE BOOK IS FULL OF HUMAN STORIES. IN FACT, SOME OF THE WORLD'S BEST STORIES ARE BETWEEN THE BIBLE'S COVERS. IT'S A BOOK TO ENJOY AND UNDERSTAND.

THE OLD TESTAMENT

THE CHRISTIAN BIBLE IS DIVIDED INTO TWO PARTS: THE OLD TESTAMENT AND THE NEW TESTAMENT.

'Testament'?

THIS WORD 'TESTAMENT' MEANS 'AGREEMENT'. THE BIBLE'S FIRST HALF REVOLVES AROUND THE AGREEMENT GOD MADE WITH ISRAEL AT MT SINAI, WHILE THE SECOND HALF REVOLVES AROUND THE AGREEMENT GOD MADE AVAILABLE TO ALL PEOPLE THROUGH THE DEATH OF JESUS CHRIST.

The Old Testament and New Testament are very different...

THE OLD TESTAMENT

Featuring: MOSES ON MT SINAI

THE NEW TESTAMENT

Featuring: THE DEATH AND RESURRECTION OF JESUS CHRIST

BOTH BOOKS ARE ACTUALLY A COLLECTION OF SMALLER BOOKS. INSIDE THE OLD TESTAMENT ARE THIRTY-NINE OF THESE BOOKS. THE NEW TESTAMENT IS SMALLER, WITH ONLY TWENTY-SEVEN. THE OLD TESTAMENT COVERS A PERIOD OF ALMOST 2,000 YEARS, WHILE THE NEW WAS WRITTEN IN A SIXTY TO SEVENTY YEAR PERIOD.

THE OLD TESTAMENT ISN'T ONE LONG BORING BIT OF WRITING. IT CONTAINS AN AMAZING VARIETY OF STUFF WRITTEN BY MANY DIFFERENT AUTHORS...

☐ STORIES — JOSEPH AND HIS COAT, QUEEN ESTHER'S COURAGE, DAVID AND GOLIATH, ETC.

☐ SONGS — THERE ARE VICTORY SONGS AFTER BATTLE, A LOVE SONG, PSALMS PRAISING GOD, LAMENTS AFTER TRAGEDY...

☐ LAWS — THE LAWS COVER ALL AREAS OF LIFE: PAYING FAIR WAGES, HOW TO TREAT FOREIGNERS, HOW TO WORSHIP GOD, ETC.

☐ PHILOSOPHY — SOME BOOKS ASK THE DEEPEST QUESTIONS OF LIFE.

☐ RIDDLES AND PROVERBS — OTHER PARTS OF THE OLD TESTAMENT GIVE SHREWD ADVICE ON HOW TO LIVE.

ALTHOUGH THE OLD TESTAMENT IS FULL OF SUCH VARIETY, ITS COMMON THEME IS THE RELATIONSHIP BETWEEN GOD AND THE ANCIENT NATION OF ISRAEL. ONE PROPHET, HOSEA, SAW THIS RELATIONSHIP AS A MARRIAGE —

Israel, I will make you my wife; I will be true and faithful...

GOD SPEAKING AS A HUSBAND IN HOSEA 2:19

BUT IT WASN'T A SENTIMENTAL, VIOLINS-PLAYING-IN-THE-BACKGROUND MARRIAGE. IT WENT THROUGH MANY QUARRELS AND ROCKY PATCHES, NEARLY ENDING UP IN DIVORCE. THE OLD TESTAMENT FOLLOWS THIS LOVE STORY WITH PAINFUL HONESTY.

Yes, yes, yes — but it's still a big book! Isn't there any way to make it more digestible?

YES, THERE IS. THE OLD TESTAMENT BREAKS DOWN INTO SEVERAL BLOCKS...

THE LAW
(GENESIS TO DEUTERONOMY) The heart of this block is the agreement and Law God gave Moses on Mt Sinai. See page 20.

HISTORY
(JOSHUA TO ESTHER) Tells the story of God's people. See page 35.

POETRY + WISDOM
(JOB TO SOLOMON'S SONG) Songs, poems, proverbs, questions about life. See page 55.

THE PROPHETS
(ISAIAH TO MALACHI) God's messengers speak out to the nation... See page 65.

ALTHOUGH THE PROPHETS COME AFTER THE HISTORY IN THE ORDER OF BOOKS IN THE OLD TESTAMENT, THEY ACTUALLY SPOKE DURING THE TIME COVERED BY THE HISTORY BOOKS. EACH PROPHET SLOTS INTO A PARTICULAR TIME IN ISRAEL'S HISTORY.

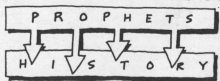

NEW TESTAMENT

THE OLD TESTAMENT CAME ABOUT THROUGH A LONG, SLOW PROCESS STRETCHING OVER MANY CENTURIES. BUT THE NEW TESTAMENT WAS QUITE THE OPPOSITE. IT WAS SET IN MOTION BY A CATACLYSMIC EVENT THAT HAPPENED AROUND THE YEAR AD 30. THIS EVENT DETONATED AN EXPLOSION OF ACTIVITY THAT STARTED A GROUP OF PEOPLE JOURNEYING, PREACHING, AND WRITING THE DOCUMENTS THAT WERE EVENTUALLY COLLECTED TO FORM THE NEW TESTAMENT.

> Fascinating. But what was this cataclysm?

THE PREACHING, MIRACLES, DEATH AND RESURRECTION OF JESUS. THIS HAPPENED OVER A THREE-YEAR PERIOD — AND YET THOSE BRIEF THREE YEARS RADICALLY CHANGED THE WORLD.

New and Old

> So when the New Testament came along, did that mean the Old Testament didn't matter any more?

> Yeah. Did it <u>replace</u> it?

NOT AT ALL. THE NEW TESTAMENT WRITERS BELIEVED THAT JESUS HAD COME AS THE FULFILLMENT AND COMPLETION OF THE FAITH OF THE OLD TESTAMENT. HE DIDN'T REPLACE THE OLD TESTAMENT, RATHER HE GAVE IT GREATER DEPTH AND MEANING. IN HIS ACCOUNT OF JESUS' LIFE, LUKE RECORDS JESUS' ATTITUDE TO THE OLD TESTAMENT...

Beginning with Moses and all the Prophets, Jesus explained to them what was said in all the Scriptures concerning himself.

LUKE 24:27

So why was it all written?

AFTER THE DEATH AND RESURRECTION OF JESUS, THE FIRST CHRISTIANS STARTED TO TRAVEL AND PREACH THE GOOD NEWS. PEOPLE HEARD THE MESSAGE BY WORD OF MOUTH — NOTHING HAD YET BEEN WRITTEN DOWN, SO ALL THEY KNEW ABOUT JESUS CAME FROM THESE FIRST PREACHERS. BUT AS TIME WENT ON AND THAT GENERATION GREW OLDER, THEY REALIZED THE NEED TO PUT THINGS DOWN IN WRITING.

THE FIRST PERSON TO REALIZE THIS WAS THE APOSTLE PAUL. HE STARTED TO WRITE LETTERS TO SOME OF THE CHURCHES HE HAD HELPED TO START. HE TOLD THEM HOW THEY SHOULD LIVE AS CHRISTIANS, AND TAUGHT THEM WHAT TO BELIEVE. HE ALSO WARNED THEM AGAINST FALSE TEACHINGS THAT HAD ALREADY STARTED TO INFEST THE CHURCH. OTHER WRITERS LIKE PETER, JAMES AND JOHN SOON FOLLOWED HIS EXAMPLE.

But will they remember it all when I've gone?

So the letters of Paul — like 1+2 Thessalonians, for example — are the earliest Christian writings we have?

Right!

AT THE SAME TIME, OTHER PEOPLE SAW THAT THE CHURCH NEEDED AN ACCURATE ACCOUNT OF THE LIFE OF JESUS. SO MARK (PROBABLY THE FIRST ONE TO DO IT) WROTE DOWN THE STORIES PETER PREACHED ABOUT WHAT JESUS HAD SAID AND DONE. AND THEN LUKE INTERVIEWED MANY OF THE PEOPLE WHO HAD KNOWN JESUS PERSONALLY, IN PUTTING HIS LIFE OF JESUS TOGETHER. IN THIS WAY, THE NEW TESTAMENT GRADUALLY CAME INTO BEING.

LIKE THE OLD TESTAMENT, IT'S MADE UP OF DIFFERENT SECTIONS...

THE GOOD NEWS
(MATTHEW - ACTS)
The story of Jesus and the Apostles. See page 90.

THE LETTERS
(ROMANS - JUDE)
Written to the young church. See page 118.

THE APOCALYPSE
(REVELATION)
Visions of the future. See page 152.

CRASH COURSE

Did you know the Bible has no fewer than 1189 chapters? So where on earth do I start? It sounds like a tall order to me...

Right!

THIS CRASH COURSE IS DESIGNED TO HELP YOU GET STARTED IN THE BIBLE. OR IF YOU'RE STUCK, TO HELP YOU GET RE-STARTED. IT INTRODUCES THIRTY SIGNIFICANT BIBLE PASSAGES THAT WILL TAKE YOU QUICKLY FROM GENESIS TO REVELATION. OBVIOUSLY IT CAN'T COVER EVERYTHING, BUT IT SHOULD GIVE YOU A TASTE FOR WHAT THE BIBLE IS ABOUT...

Just think. If you read one a day, it'll take you a month.

Unless it's February.

---

1 'Let there be light!'
Genesis 1:1– 2:4

THE BIBLE OPENS WITH A MAJESTIC DESCRIPTION OF GOD AS CREATOR OF EVERYTHING. HUMANKIND IS SEEN AS THE PEAK OF GOD'S CREATION.

2 The Garden of Eden
Genesis 2:5– 3:24

THIS SECOND CREATION ACCOUNT FOCUSES ON ADAM AND EVE. CHAPTER 3 DESCRIBES 'THE FALL', WHEN GOD'S GOOD CREATION WAS SPOILED (SEE PAGE 22).

3 God tests Abraham
Genesis 22:1–19

ABRAHAM (SEE PAGE 24) WAS THE FATHER OF THE JEWISH RACE. HERE GOD TESTS HIS LOYALTY TO HIM SEVERELY.

4 The burning bush
Exodus 2–3

CENTURIES AFTER ABRAHAM, THE JEWS WERE SLAVES IN EGYPT. MOSES (SEE PAGE 30) IS HERE CALLED BY GOD TO HELP FREE THE SLAVES.

5 The great escape
Exodus 14

THE JEWISH SLAVES HAVE BEEN SET FREE. BUT THEY ARE PURSUED AND TRAPPED AGAINST THE SEA (SEE PAGE 28).

6 At Mt Sinai
Exodus 19:1–20:21

MOSES' PEOPLE REACH THIS MOUNTAIN IN THE DESERT. HERE GOD MAKES A 'COVENANT' (AGREEMENT) WITH THEM AND GIVES THEM HIS LAW.

7 'Be holy...'
Leviticus 19

IN THIS CHAPTER OF LAWS, GOD WANTS HIS PEOPLE TO REFLECT HIS CHARACTER. THE LAWS HAVE A SPECIAL CONCERN FOR THE POOR AND POWERLESS.

8 David meets Goliath
1 Samuel 17

OVER 200 YEARS AFTER MOSES, THE NATION OF ISRAEL IS UNDER THREAT FROM ITS ENEMIES, THE PHILISTINES (SEE PAGES 44-45).

9 Elijah and the fire
1 Kings 18

100 YEARS AFTER DAVID'S DEATH, ISRAEL IS AGAIN UNDER THREAT — THIS TIME FROM THE WORSHIP OF FALSE GODS (SEE PAGE 48).

10 Elisha and Naaman
2 Kings 5

ELISHA WAS SUCCESSOR TO ELIJAH (SEE PAGE 49). IN THIS EPISODE, GOD'S CONCERN AND CARE FOR NON-JEWS COMES ACROSS.

11 God the Shepherd
Psalm 23

THE BEST-KNOWN OF ALL THE PSALMS. THIS PICTURE OF GOD AS A SHEPHERD WAS ECHOED BY JESUS IN JOHN 10:1-18.

12 David's repentance
Psalm 51

2 SAMUEL 11:1-12:23 IS THE HISTORICAL BACKGROUND TO THIS PSALM. DAVID DESPERATELY SEEKS GOD'S FORGIVENESS.

13 Wise sayings
Proverbs 23

A CHAPTER FULL OF STRAIGHTFORWARD ADVICE ABOUT PRACTICAL LIVING. THIS CHAPTER IS TYPICAL OF THE BOOK OF PROVERBS.

14 Isaiah's call
Isaiah 6

ISAIAH (SEE PAGES 68-69) SEES GOD, HAS HIS SINS FORGIVEN, AND IS SENT AS A PROPHET TO ISRAEL.

15 'Comfort my people'
Isaiah 40

THESE WORDS WERE WRITTEN TO ENCOURAGE THE JEWS IN EXILE (SEE PAGES 74-75). IT GIVES A VIVID PICTURE OF THE ALL-POWERFUL GOD.

16 The Suffering Servant
Isaiah 52:13 – 53:12

OVER 500 YEARS BEFORE JESUS SUFFERED AND DIED, ISAIAH PROPHESIED ABOUT GOD'S SERVANT WHO SUFFERED FOR MANKIND.

17 Valley of Dry Bones
Ezekiel 37:1-14

EZEKIEL'S STRANGE VISION IS PARTLY ABOUT THE REVIVAL OF ISRAEL AS A NATION AFTER THE EXILE (SEE PAGE 73).

18 Daniel in the Lions' Den
Daniel 6

IN THE EXILE, DANIEL REACHED A POWERFUL POSITION IN THE BABYLONIAN ROYAL COURT (SEE PAGES 76-77). HERE HIS FAITH IS TESTED.

19 Sermon on the Mount
Matthew 5-7

THIS IS THE MOST FAMOUS BLOCK OF JESUS' TEACHING. IN IT HE SHOWS HOW HIS FOLLOWERS SHOULD LIVE OUT THE NEW LIFE OF GOD'S KINGDOM.

20 Jesus the healer
Mark 5

IN THREE STORIES, JESUS' POWER OVER EVIL, DISEASE AND DEATH IS DRAMATICALLY SEEN IN ACTION.

21 Jesus is crucified
Mark 14-15

THE PLOTS OF JESUS' ENEMIES FINALLY REACH A CLIMAX. BUT HIS DEATH IS NO ACCIDENT. IT IS PART OF GOD'S PLAN AND IT IS WHAT JESUS CAME FOR.

22 'He is risen!'
Luke 24

THESE STORIES ARE AT THE HEART OF THE CHRISTIAN FAITH. JESUS APPEARS TO HIS FOLLOWERS AS THE DESTROYER OF DEATH.

23 Washing feet
John 13

JOHN ALONE RECORDS THIS INCIDENT WHEN JESUS SHOWED THAT HE HAD COME AS A SERVANT.

24 The Day of Pentecost
Acts 2

SEVEN WEEKS AFTER JESUS' RESURRECTION, THE FIRST CHRISTIANS WERE FILLED WITH THE POWER OF THE HOLY SPIRIT (SEE PAGE 114).

25 Paul's conversion
Acts 9:1-31

PAUL, VIOLENT PERSECUTOR OF CHRISTIANS, IS DRAMATICALLY CONVERTED (SEE PAGE 127).

26 The storm at sea
Acts 27

PAUL IS ON HIS WAY TO ROME, WHERE HE FACES TRIAL BEFORE THE EMPEROR. THIS STORM SHOWS HOW HE ACTED UNDER PRESSURE (SEE PAGE 125).

27 Love
1 Corinthians 13

PAUL WROTE THIS LETTER TO A CHURCH TORN APART BY PRIDE. THIS FAMOUS PASSAGE SHOWS WHAT THEIR FIRST PRIORITY SHOULD BE.

28 Christian living
Ephesians 5-6

PAUL SHOWS HOW CHRISTIANS SHOULD LIVE IN THE MIDST OF A HOSTILE WORLD.

29 Christ, first-born Son
Colossians 1:15-23

THIS PASSAGE SPELLS OUT THE TRUE IDENTITY OF JESUS CHRIST. AS HEAD OF GOD'S NEW CREATION, HE RECONCILES PEOPLE TO GOD.

30 New heaven, new earth
Revelation 21-22

THE BIBLE CLOSES WITH THE RE-CREATION OF THE UNIVERSE BY GOD. HIS REDEMPTION OF THE EFFECTS OF SIN AND DEATH IS COMPLETE.

THE LAW

This section contains the books of...

Genesis, Exodus, Leviticus, Numbers and Deuteronomy

THE LAW

FOR THE JEWISH PEOPLE, THE LAW WAS AT THE HEART OF THE OLD TESTAMENT. A QUICK LOOK AT THESE QUOTES SHOWS WHAT THEY THOUGHT ABOUT THEIR LAW...

The Law of the Lord is perfect; it gives new strength

PSALM 19

How I love your Law! I think about it all day long!

PSALM 119

If a man studies the Law, he comes to know the will of God

A JEWISH RABBI

BUT WHAT IS THE LAW?

WHEN JEWS TALKED ABOUT THE LAW, THEY REALLY MEANT 'THE LAW OF MOSES'. THIS IS THE FIRST FIVE BOOKS OF THE BIBLE, WHICH WERE TRADITIONALLY BELIEVED TO HAVE BEEN WRITTEN BY MOSES.

THE LAW = GENESIS, EXODUS, LEVITICUS, NUMBERS AND DEUTERONOMY

THESE 'BOOKS OF MOSES' AREN'T JUST FULL OF RULES AND REGULATIONS. THEY CONTAIN EPIC STORIES, AT LEAST A COUPLE OF SONGS, BATTLE ACCOUNTS, AND THE FAMOUS CREATION STORY OF GENESIS.

SO WHY CALL THEM 'THE LAW'?

BECAUSE THE FOCUS OF THE BOOKS IS THE EVENT WHEN GOD GAVE HIS LAW TO MOSES ON MT SINAI. HE REVEALED HIMSELF TO HIS PEOPLE AND SHOWED THEM HOW THEY SHOULD LIVE.

THE BOOK OF GENESIS IS FAIRLY EASY TO READ AS IT IS FULL OF ACTION. BUT EXODUS, LEVITICUS, NUMBERS AND DEUTERONOMY ARE HARDER – THE STORYLINE IS MIXED IN WITH VARIOUS BLOCKS OF LAWS. HERE'S HOW TO SORT IT ALL OUT...

FOLLOWING THE STORY

- <u>EXODUS 1–20</u> TELLS THE STORY OF THE ESCAPE FROM EGYPT
- <u>EXODUS 24</u> THE AGREEMENT ON MT SINAI IS SEALED
- <u>EXODUS 32–34</u> THE PEOPLE WORSHIP A GOLDEN BULL AND THE COVENANT HAS TO BE RENEWED
- <u>EXODUS 40</u> THE TENT WHERE GOD IS TO BE WORSHIPPED IS SET UP
- <u>NUMBERS 9–14</u> THEY LEAVE SINAI AND BEGIN TO COMPLAIN AGAINST MOSES
- <u>NUMBERS 16–17</u> REBELLION AGAINST MOSES BREAKS OUT
- <u>NUMBERS 20–24</u> THEY MEET WITH SUCCESS ON THE EDGE OF THE PROMISED LAND
- <u>DEUTERONOMY 31 + 34</u> BECAUSE HE DISOBEYED GOD, MOSES CAN'T ENTER THE PROMISED LAND

FINDING THE LAWS

- <u>EXODUS 20:1–17</u> THE TEN COMMANDMENTS
- <u>EXODUS 21–23</u> CALLED 'THE BOOK OF THE COVENANT', IT GIVES LOTS OF DIFFERENT LAWS
- <u>LEVITICUS</u> THIS BOOK IS FULL OF LAWS (SEE PAGE 31)
- <u>DEUTERONOMY</u> THIS WORD MEANS 'THE SECOND LAW' – THE LAW HAD TO BE RE-TOLD TO ISRAEL (SEE PAGE 34)

But what do all these laws mean? Do we have to keep them today – or do we just ignore them?

Yeah. Should I stop eating pork, start sacrificing animals, etc?

HERE ARE THREE THINGS TO THINK ABOUT...

1 THE LAWS SHOW US WHAT GOD IS LIKE. SO IT'S GOOD TO READ THEM TO FIND OUT MORE ABOUT GOD.

2 MANY OF THE LAWS (E.G. ABOUT FOOD) WERE FOR THAT TIME ONLY. BUT OTHERS, LIKE THE TEN COMMANDMENTS, ARE DIRECTLY RELEVANT TO US TODAY.

3 ALTHOUGH THE ISRAELITES WERE GIVEN THE LAW, THEY DIDN'T HAVE THE POWER TO LIVE UP TO IT. THIS ONLY CAME WITH JESUS. (SEE PAGES 128 + 129 FOR MORE ON THIS.)

21

GENESIS

'GENESIS' IS A GREEK WORD THAT LITERALLY MEANS 'ORIGINS'. WE GET 'GENERATE', 'GENES' AND 'GENEALOGY' FROM THE SAME ROOT WORD. THE BOOK OF GENESIS COULD JUST AS EASILY BE TITLED 'ORIGINS'. IT TRACES ORIGINS IN TWO WAYS:

THE ORIGIN OF THE HUMAN RACE (GENESIS 1-11)

THE ORIGIN OF THE PEOPLE OF GOD (GENESIS 12-50)

GENESIS 1-11 INCLUDES SOME FAMOUS STORIES —

- ❑ THE CREATION GENESIS 1
- ❑ THE GARDEN OF EDEN GENESIS 2-3
- ❑ THE FIRST MURDER GENESIS 4
- ❑ THE GREAT FLOOD GENESIS 6-9
- ❑ THE TOWER OF BABEL GENESIS 11

Yes, but am I expected to believe in a seven-day creation of the universe, Adam and Eve, talking animals, the Garden of Eden, a world-wide flood, kangaroos on the ark and all the rest?

SOME CHRISTIANS WOULD SAY YES. THE DESCRIPTIONS IN THE EARLY CHAPTERS OF GENESIS ARE LITERAL, HISTORICAL EVENTS.

OTHER CHRISTIANS BELIEVE THAT THE WRITER OR WRITERS OF THESE CHAPTERS WERE USING PICTURE LANGUAGE TO EXPLAIN, IN TERMS EVERYONE CAN UNDERSTAND, WHAT GOD IS LIKE.

THEN THERE ARE A HOST OF VIEWS IN BETWEEN. BUT MOST SIGNIFICANT IS THE FACT THAT THE BIBLE OPENS BY FACING THE DEEPEST HUMAN QUESTIONS: WHO MADE US? DOES LIFE HAVE MEANING? WHY IS NOBODY PERFECT? IS THERE A GOD? IF SO, WHAT DOES HE DO AND WHAT IS HE LIKE? AND DOES HE CARE ABOUT WHAT HAPPENS IN OUR WORLD?

THE STORY OF GENESIS 12-50 FOCUSES ON FOUR PEOPLE —

FOUR PEOPLE, EH? WHAT WERE THEIR NAMES?

THEY WERE ABRAM (LATER CALLED <u>ABRAHAM</u>), ISAAC, JACOB AND JOSEPH. ISAAC WAS ABRAHAM'S SON, JACOB WAS ISAAC'S SON, AND SO ON.

NOW, FOR THE LAST TIME, HAVE YOU GOT MY SANDWICHES?

ABRAHAM

ABRAHAM APPEARS IN GENESIS 11-25. GOD PROMISED HIM THAT HIS DESCENDANTS WOULD BECOME GOD'S CHOSEN PEOPLE — A NATION HE WOULD USE FOR GOOD IN THE WORLD. GENESIS CHARTS THE STORY OF THE FIRST FOUR GENERATIONS OF THIS NATION. FOR MORE ON ABRAHAM, SEE PAGE 24.

ISAAC

YOU CAN READ ISAAC'S STORY IN GENESIS 21 - 35. HE WAS THE FATHER OF TWO QUARRELSOME SONS: JACOB AND ESAU.

JACOB

JACOB IS IN GENESIS 25-49. HE HAD TWELVE SONS (BY FOUR DIFFERENT WOMEN). IN TIME, THEY BECAME THE TWELVE TRIBES OF ISRAEL.

JACOB WAS THE ONE WHO WRESTLED WITH GOD IN GENESIS CHAPTER 32.

JOSEPH

JOSEPH (GENESIS 37-50) WAS SOLD BY HIS BROTHERS AS AN EGYPTIAN SLAVE. BUT GOD SAW TO IT THAT JOSEPH BECAME PRIME MINISTER OF ALL EGYPT...

> ALSO KNOWN AS ABRAM!

ABRAHAM

> ABRAHAM — WHO WAS HE?.

> WELL, ABRAHAM LIVED ABOUT 1900 BC AND WAS REVERED BY ALL THE JEWS BECAUSE HE WAS THE FATHER OF THE WHOLE JEWISH PEOPLE.

> YES, BUT WHAT DID HE DO?

> YOU CAN READ HIS STORY, STARTING AT GENESIS 12. HE HAD GREAT FAITH IN GOD AND LEFT THE SECURITY OF HIS HOME TO OBEY HIM. ALTHOUGH HE AND SARAH HIS WIFE WERE OLD, ABRAHAM STILL BELIEVED GOD WOULD GIVE HIM A SON AND MAKE HIM THE FATHER OF MANY PEOPLE.

KEY EVENTS

WHERE TO READ ABOUT ABRAHAM...

■ GOD CALLS ABRAM TO CANAAN — GENESIS 12:1-9

■ ABRAM RESCUES HIS NEPHEW, LOT — GENESIS 14

■ GOD'S AGREEMENT WITH ABRAM — GENESIS 15

■ GOD PROMISES ABRAHAM AND SARAH A SON — GENESIS 18:1-15

■ SODOM AND GOMORRAH — GENESIS 18:16-19:29

■ ISAAC IS BORN — GENESIS 21:1-8

■ GOD TESTS ABRAHAM — GENESIS 22

■ ABRAHAM DIES — GENESIS 25:7-11

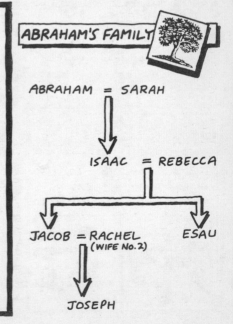

ABRAHAM'S FAMILY

ABRAHAM = SARAH

ISAAC = REBECCA

JACOB = RACHEL (WIFE No. 2)   ESAU

JOSEPH

PROMISED LAND

ABRAHAM AND HIS FAMILY WERE NOMADS. THEY DIDN'T HAVE A LAND OF THEIR OWN TO LIVE IN, BUT TRAVELLED ABOUT IN SEARCH OF FRESH PASTURES FOR THEIR ANIMALS. THEY LIVED IN TENTS. THIS WAY OF LIFE HAD ITS OWN DIFFICULTIES...

> Yeah! It's no joke trying to kick-start your camel on a cold morning!

ALTHOUGH THE NOMAD LIFE WAS GOOD FOR ABRAHAM, ISAAC AND JACOB, IT COULDN'T GO ON FOR EVER, ESPECIALLY IF ABRAHAM'S DESCENDANTS WERE TO GROW TO THE SIZE OF A NATION.

SO GOD PROMISED ABRAHAM THE LAND OF CANAAN AS THE HOME FOR HIS PEOPLE — ALTHOUGH IT WOULD BE HUNDREDS OF YEARS BEFORE THEY FINALLY OCCUPIED IT. THIS IS WHY IT WAS CALLED THE 'PROMISED' LAND. IT WAS PROMISED TO THEM BY GOD, EVEN IF IT WASN'T YET THEIRS.

600 YEARS AFTER ABRAHAM, HIS DESCENDANTS STILL HADN'T RECEIVED THE LAND PROMISED THEM. IN FACT, THEY WERE NOW SLAVES IN EGYPT. BUT MOSES PROMISED THAT GOD STILL PLANNED TO LEAD THEM TO CANAAN — A LAND SO FERTILE THAT IT 'FLOWED WITH MILK + HONEY'.

> Look carefully in all directions. I am going to give you and all your descendants all the land that you see, and it will be yours for ever.

GOD'S PROMISE TO ABRAM IN GENESIS 13:15

25

EXODUS

'EXODUS', LIKE THE WORD 'EXIT' MEANS 'GOING OUT'. THE BOOK IS GIVEN THIS TITLE BECAUSE IT TELLS THE GREATEST STORY OF ISRAEL'S HISTORY — WHEN ABRAHAM'S DESCENDANTS ESCAPED FROM CRUEL SLAVERY IN EGYPT.

THE BOOK OF EXODUS DIVIDES INTO TWO PARTS...

1 The Great Escape

EXODUS 1-18

OVER 400 YEARS AFTER THE TIME OF JOSEPH, THE ISRAELITES WERE SLAVES IN EGYPT. BUT GOD HEARD THEIR CRIES FOR HELP AND CALLED MOSES TO LEAD THEM TO FREEDOM. THE EGYPTIANS DIDN'T WANT TO RELEASE THEM, AND EVEN AFTER THEY HAD ESCAPED, TRIED TO RECAPTURE THEM. (SEE PAGE 30 FOR DETAILS.)

AN EGYPTIAN KING (OR 'PHARAOH'

2 The Great Covenant

EXODUS 19-40

MOSES LEADS THE PEOPLE INTO THE DESERT. THEY REACH MT SINAI, WHICH MOSES CLIMBS TO MEET GOD. HERE GOD MAKES A 'COVENANT' (OR 'AGREEMENT') WITH HIS PEOPLE. HE GIVES THEM...

- MORAL, SOCIAL AND RELIGIOUS LAWS TO LIVE BY
- INSTRUCTIONS TO MAKE A TENT WHICH WILL BE THE FOCUS OF ISRAEL'S WORSHIP AND SACRIFICE.

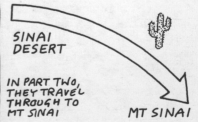

RED SEA

SINAI DESERT

EGYPT

IN PART ONE, THE ISRAELITES TRAVEL FROM EGYPT TO BEYOND THE RED SEA

IN PART TWO, THEY TRAVEL THROUGH TO MT SINAI

MT SINAI

NOT ONLY DOES EXODUS HAVE A GREAT, TRUE STORY WITH MANY FAMOUS INCIDENTS (E.G. MOSES IN THE BULLRUSHES, THE BURNING BUSH, THE RED SEA, ETC.) IT ALSO HAS ONE OF THE BEST-KNOWN SET OF LAWS IN THE WORLD: THE TEN COMMANDMENTS. THESE FAMOUS LAWS, GIVEN BY GOD TO MOSES ON MT SINAI, SUM UP WHAT GOD WANTS IN OUR RELATIONSHIPS WITH HIM AND OTHERS.

RELATIONSHIP WITH GOD
1. DON'T WORSHIP OTHER GODS.
2. DON'T MAKE IDOLS.
3. DON'T TAKE GOD'S NAME IN VAIN.
4. KEEP ONE DAY A WEEK FOR REST AND WORSHIP.

RELATIONSHIP WITH OTHERS
5. RESPECT YOUR PARENTS.
6. DON'T MURDER.
7. DON'T COMMIT ADULTERY.
8. DON'T STEAL.
9. DON'T LIE.
10. DON'T BE JEALOUS OF WHAT SOMEONE ELSE HAS GOT.

The GREAT ESCAPE

Psst! What was this Exodus thing all about?

Well, it happened in three stages—

1/ PLAGUES

THE EGYPTIAN KING REFUSED TO LET GOD'S PEOPLE LEAVE EGYPT. IN EXODUS 7-10 GOD SENDS NINE PLAGUES TO HELP HIM CHANGE HIS MIND. THEY WERE...

blood   frogs   gnats

flies

boils   animal disease

hail   locusts

darkness

I thought acne was a teenage problem until I met Moses!

AGED EGYPTIAN BOIL-SUFFERER

2/ PASSOVER

BUT THE KING STILL WOULDN'T RELENT. SO GOD TOLD MOSES TO PREPARE FOR THE PASSOVER PLAN. THIS WAS...

- AT MIDNIGHT, GOD WOULD KILL ALL THE OLDEST SONS IN EGYPT.
- THE ISRAELITES WERE TO EAT A SPECIAL MEAL, WITH LAMB. THE LAMB'S BLOOD WAS TO BE PAINTED ON THEIR DOORPOSTS OUTSIDE.
- GOD WOULD SEE THE BLOOD AND 'PASS OVER' THE HOUSE, SPARING THE ISRAELITE SONS.

AFTER THIS, THE KING LET THE ISRAELITES GO. THE PEOPLE WERE TOLD TO CELEBRATE THE PASSOVER EVERY YEAR.

3/ PLUNGE!

'OUT OF THE FRYING PAN AND INTO THE FIRE' AS THE SAYING GOES. NO SOONER WERE THEY OUT OF EGYPT THAN THE KING PURSUED THEM AND TRAPPED THEM WITH HIS ARMY AGAINST THE SEA.

They were in it up to the gills...

BUT GOD HAD A FURTHER SURPRISE IN STORE. IN EXODUS 14 HE PARTS THE SEA, ALLOWING ISRAEL TO ESCAPE, WHILE THE EGYPTIAN ARMY IS DROWNED.

LEVITICUS

WHAT'S IT ALL ABOUT?

LEVITICUS IS A BOOK THAT GIVES LAWS ABOUT HOW THE COMMUNITY OF ISRAEL SHOULD LIVE AND WORSHIP TOGETHER AS GOD'S PEOPLE. IT'S AN AMAZING COLLECTION OF LAWS THAT COVER WORSHIP, TREATMENT OF SLAVES, DATES OF FESTIVALS, PAYING FAIR WAGES, NOT MARRYING YOUR SISTER, WHAT MEATS TO EAT, AVOIDING OCCULT RELIGIONS — IN OTHER WORDS, THE BOOK COVERS THE WHOLE OF LIFE! LAWS ABOUT WORSHIP AND SACRIFICE RUB SHOULDERS WITH LAWS FOR EVERYDAY LIFE, SHOWING THAT GOD IS CONCERNED FOR THE WAY WE LIVE THE WHOLE OF OUR LIVES.

THE KEY WORDS IN THE BOOK ARE LEVITICUS 11:44

> I am the Lord your God, and you must keep yourselves holy, because I am holy.

SOME TYPICAL BITS...

LEVITICUS 19:13

Do not hold back the wages of a hired man overnight.

LEVITICUS 19:4

Do not abandon me and worship idols; do not make gods of metal and worship them.

Use honest scales and honest weights.

LEVITICUS 19:36

 OINK

Show respect for the elderly and revere your God.

LEVITICUS 19:32

Do not eat pigs. They must be considered unclean; they have divided hooves, but do not chew the cud.

LEVITICUS 11:7

29

MOSES His Life!

MOSES IS ONE OF THE GIANTS OF THE BIBLE. NO OTHER OLD TESTAMENT CHARACTER DOMINATES <u>FOUR</u> WHOLE BOOKS! MOSES WAS THE GREAT LEADER OF ISRAEL DURING THE EXODUS FROM EGYPT. BUT THE THING THAT STANDS OUT ABOUT MOSES IS HIS TENACIOUS FAITH IN GOD. WHILE EVERYONE ELSE DOUBTED OR REBELLED, MOSES SOLIDLY BELIEVED IN WHAT GOD WAS DOING. HIS LIFE FALLS INTO THREE PARTS —

EARLY

▷ MOSES WAS HIDDEN AS A BABY BECAUSE OF AN EGYPTIAN DECREE THAT ALL HEBREW BABY BOYS BE KILLED.

▷ HE WAS FOUND BY AN EGYPTIAN PRINCESS, AND BROUGHT UP IN THE ROYAL COURT.

> He was taught all the wisdom of the Egyptians, and became a great man in words and deeds.
>
> ACTS 7:22

▷ MOSES KILLED AN EGYPTIAN WHO HAD KILLED A HEBREW SLAVE. WANTED FOR MURDER, HE FLED INTO EXILE (EXODUS 2).

MIDDLE

▷ AS A SHEPHERD IN THE DESERT, MOSES SAW A BURNING BUSH. GOD SPOKE TO HIM OUT OF IT, AND CALLED HIM TO LEAD THE ISRAELITES OUT OF EGYPT (EXODUS 3).

▷ MOSES RETURNED TO EGYPT AND WENT TO THE KING, WHO REFUSED TO LET GOD'S PEOPLE GO. AFTER THE PASSOVER (SEE PAGE 28) MOSES LED THEM OUT TO FREEDOM (EXODUS 5-12).

▷ AT MT SINAI IN THE DESERT, MOSES RECEIVED THE LAW FROM GOD.

LATE

▷ THE LAST FORTY YEARS OF MOSES' LIFE WERE SPENT IN THE THANKLESS TASK OF LEADING GOD'S PEOPLE AS THEY WANDERED IN THE DESERT (SEE PAGE 32).

▷ AT ONE CRUCIAL POINT, MOSES DISOBEYED GOD. BECAUSE OF THIS, HE WAS BARRED FROM ENTERING THE PROMISED LAND (NUMBERS 20:1-13).

▷ AFTER MOSES, JOSHUA LED ISRAEL (DEUTERONOMY 31).

> There never has been a prophet in Israel like Moses; the Lord spoke with him face to face.
>
> DEUTERONOMY 34:10

12 TRIBES

I keep reading here about these 'Twelve Tribes of Israel'. What's it about?

THE NATION OF ISRAEL WAS MADE UP OF TWELVE FAMILIES, EACH DESCENDED FROM ONE OF THE SONS OF JACOB (WHO WAS HIMSELF THE GRANDSON OF ABRAHAM AND SARAH). THESE TWELVE FAMILIES WERE THE TWELVE TRIBES.

IN A VERY REAL SENSE, GOD WAS THEIR RULER. THEY DIDN'T HAVE A KING AND THEIR LEADERS WERE APPOINTED BY GOD. THIS WAS A UNIQUE ARRANGEMENT AND IT MEANT THAT ISRAEL WAS 'GOD'S PEOPLE'.

But who ruled them?

THE TWELVE TRIBES ARE IN THE SPOTLIGHT IN THE BIBLE SEVERAL TIMES...

 AFTER THE EXODUS FROM EGYPT, MOSES CARRIED OUT A CENSUS AT MT SINAI (NUMBERS 1-4). THE TRIBES WERE GIVEN SPECIAL PLACES TO CAMP (AROUND THE TENT USED TO WORSHIP GOD), AND SPECIAL MARCHING ORDERS FOR WHEN THEY WERE ON THE MOVE.

 WHEN THE NATION ENTERED THE PROMISED LAND, EACH TRIBE WAS GIVEN ITS OWN PIECE OF TERRITORY TO SETTLE (JOSHUA 13-21).

 IN THE TIME OF THE JUDGES, THERE WAS OFTEN FRICTION BETWEEN THE TRIBES. SOME TRIBES WERE LAZIER THAN OTHERS WHEN IT CAME TO UNITE AND FIGHT A COMMON ENEMY (JUDGES 5: 13-18).

 THIS FRICTION LED TO THE INFAMOUS (AND IRREVERSIBLE) SPLIT BETWEEN THE TEN NORTHERN TRIBES AND THE TWO SOUTHERN ONES AFTER THE REIGN OF KING SOLOMON (1 KINGS 11-12). FROM THEN ON, THE NORTH WAS CALLED ISRAEL, AND THE SOUTH, JUDAH.

NUMBERS

WHAT? YOU MEAN 32, 106, 29, 522, 1912 ...?

<u>NO!</u> THE <u>BOOK</u> OF NUMBERS. SO-CALLED BECAUSE IN IT MOSES COUNTED ALL THE PEOPLE OF ISRAEL IN THE DESERT.

NUMBERS PICKS UP THE STORY OF THE ESCAPED ISRAELITE SLAVES FROM WHERE IT LEFT OFF AT THE END OF EXODUS. ON THEIR WAY ACROSS THE DESERT TO THE PROMISED LAND, THE PEOPLE KEEP REBELLING AGAINST MOSES AND COMPLAINING AT GOD. THE CRISIS OF THE BOOK HAPPENS WHEN GOD SAYS...

You will die here in this wilderness. Your children will wander in the wilderness for forty years, suffering for your unfaithfulness, until the last one of you dies.

NUMBERS 14:32-33

So how does the book work?

LIKE THIS...

- ☐ THE PEOPLE GET READY AND THEN LEAVE MT SINAI (NUMBERS 1-10).
- ☐ THEY MOAN ABOUT THE POOR FOOD — GOD SENDS THEM QUAIL (NUMBERS 11).
- ☐ TWELVE SPIES ARE SENT ON A MISSION INTO THE PROMISED LAND. TEN BRING BACK A BAD REPORT AND THE PEOPLE REFUSE TO ENTER THE LAND. THEY REBEL AGAINST MOSES. GOD CONDEMNS THEM TO WANDER IN THE DESERT FOR FORTY YEARS (NUMBERS 13-14).
- ☐ NUMBERS 15-19 COVER THIRTY-EIGHT MISERABLE YEARS OF WANDERING IN THE DESERT.
- ☐ AT LAST ISRAEL IS ON THE MOVE — BUT THE KING OF EDOM REFUSES TO LET THEM CROSS HIS LAND. SO THEY GO ON TO MOAB, DEFEATING KINGS SIHON AND OG (NUMBERS 20-21).
- ☐ THE KING OF MOAB TRIES TO GET BALAAM (A RENT-A-PROPHET) TO CURSE ISRAEL. INSTEAD, HE BLESSES THEM (NUMBERS 22-24).

You refuse to curse the people of Israel, but at least don't bless them!

KING OF MOAB TO BALAAM

JOSEPH

JOSEPH'S STORY IN THE BOOK OF GENESIS IS ONE OF THE MOST GRIPPING AND SURPRISING IN THE BIBLE. THIS CHART GIVES A SMALL IDEA OF THE UPS AND DOWNS OF JOSEPH'S CAREER. THE STORY CAN BE FOUND IN GENESIS 37 AND 39 – 47.

JOSEPH'S PROGRESS

Prime Minister Joseph is made ruler, under the king, of all Egypt.

Eleventh son Joseph is born when Jacob his father is old.

Spoiled kid Jacob loves Joseph more than his other children. And Joseph's actions make his brothers jealous.

King's interpreter The King of Egypt has a strange dream that no one can interpret. But Joseph's reputation reaches the king. He is brought from prison and correctly interprets the dream.

Potiphar's servant In Egypt, Joseph is sold to the Captain of the Palace Guard. He is made Potiphar's personal servant.

Egyptian slave Ten of the brothers plot to kill Joseph, but at the last minute they sell him as a slave to traders.

Dream-interpreter In prison, Joseph interprets two fellow-prisoners' dreams.

Wrongly imprisoned But Potiphar's wife tries to seduce Joseph. He refuses her advances, she claims he tried to rape her and he is thrown into prison.

JOSEPH WENT ON TO SAVE THE WORLD OF HIS TIME FROM FAMINE. AND HE TOLD HIS BROTHERS, WHO HAD SOLD HIM INTO SLAVERY...

God sent me ahead of you to rescue you in this amazing way and to make sure that you and your descendants survive.

Genesis 45:7

DEUTERONOMY

THIS IS WHAT THE BOOK OF DEUTERONOMY REALLY IS — A COLLECTION OF MOSES' GREAT SPEECHES GIVEN JUST BEFORE THE PEOPLE OF ISRAEL ENTERED THE PROMISED LAND (AFTER FORTY YEARS TREKKING THROUGH THE DESERT). THE SPEECHES REMIND THE PEOPLE OF GOD'S LOVE AND FAITHFULNESS AND ARE A ROUSING CALL TO BE FAITHFUL TO HIM IN RETURN. DEUTERONOMY IS A KIND OF 'MOSES' GREATEST HITS'...

YOU ARE INVITED
to hear
· **MOSES** ·
GIVING A SERIES OF FINAL SPEECHES
PLACE   ON THE PLAINS OF MOAB
TIME   ABOUT 1260 BC
The speeches will be followed by the triumphant entry of Israel into the Promised land.
BRING YOUR OWN SWORD!

M·O·S·E·S
ALL · TIME · GREATS

SPEECH 1 MOSES RECALLS ALL THAT GOD DID FOR HIS PEOPLE IN THE DESERT. HE SUMS UP: 'THE LORD IS GOD IN HEAVEN AND EARTH. THERE IS NO OTHER GOD. OBEY ALL HIS LAWS... AND ALL WILL GO WELL WITH YOU' (DEUT. 1–4).

SPEECH 2 MOSES PREACHES ON THE TEN COMMANDMENTS. THE MOST FAMOUS WORDS OF THE WHOLE BOOK COME HERE: 'HEAR, O ISRAEL! THE LORD OUR GOD, THE LORD IS ONE. LOVE THE LORD YOUR GOD WITH ALL YOUR HEART..' JESUS SAID THESE WORDS WERE THE GREATEST LAW OF THE OLD TESTAMENT (DEUT. 5–26).

SPEECH 3 MOSES OUTLINES THE CURSES IF THE PEOPLE DISOBEY GOD, AND THE BLESSINGS IF THEY OBEY (DEUT. 27–28).

MOSES' SONG NO SWEET SONG THIS, INSTEAD A SERIES OF SAVAGE WARNINGS ABOUT THE PERILS OF ABANDONING GOD (DEUT. 32).

SPEECH 4 MOSES APPEALS TO THEM TO STICK BY THEIR COMMITMENT TO GOD. 'TODAY I AM GIVING YOU A CHOICE BETWEEN GOOD AND EVIL, BETWEEN LIFE AND DEATH' (DEUT. 29–30).

MOSES' BLESSINGS THE FINAL WORDS OF MOSES ARE TO BLESS EACH OF THE TRIBES OF ISRAEL (EXCEPT SIMEON, LATER ABSORBED INTO JUDAH) DEUT. 33.

HISTORY BOOKS

THIS SECTION CONTAINS THE BOOKS OF...

JOSHUA, JUDGES, RUTH
1 + 2 SAMUEL, 1 + 2 KINGS,
1 + 2 CHRONICLES, EZRA,
NEHEMIAH AND ESTHER

History Books

THESE HISTORY BOOKS SOUND A BIT HEAVY. HAVE I GOT TO READ THEM?

NO, YOU HAVEN'T. BUT IF YOU IGNORE THEM, YOU'LL MISS SOME OF THE BEST MOMENTS OF THE BIBLE. IN THE BOX BELOW ARE SEVEN OF THE 'GREAT' PASSAGES FROM THESE HISTORY BOOKS. YOU COULD TRY READING ONE EACH DAY FOR A WEEK AS A WAY OF GETTING INTO THE STORIES OF THE OLD TESTAMENT...

So what exactly are these history books about?

7 STORIES

1 THE WALLS OF JERICHO COLLAPSE JOSHUA 2 + 6

2 GIDEON DEFEATS ISRAEL'S ENEMIES JUDGES 6-7

3 DAVID AND GOLIATH 1 SAMUEL 17

4 DAVID AND BATHSHEBA 2 SAMUEL 11-12

5 SOLOMON PRAYS FOR WISDOM 1 KINGS 3

6 ELIJAH DEFEATS THE PRIESTS OF THE FALSE GOD, BAAL 1 KINGS 18-19

7 ELISHA THE PROPHET HEALS NAAMAN 2 KINGS 5

The twelve books that are in this section of the Bible tell the story of God's people over about 800 years. It's a story with many ups and downs. The Israelites started as a bunch of runaway slaves from Egypt, stranded in the desert. They conquered the Promised Land and became a powerful nation. But because they abandoned their faith in God, they were once again taken into slavery in a foreign land.

The chart on the next page gives an outline of the story...

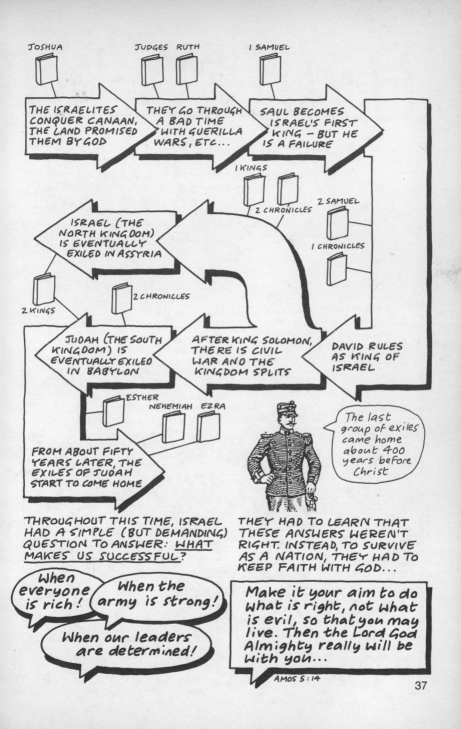

JOSHUA

JUDGES RUTH

1 SAMUEL

THE ISRAELITES CONQUER CANAAN, THE LAND PROMISED THEM BY GOD

THEY GO THROUGH A BAD TIME WITH GUERILLA WARS, ETC...

SAUL BECOMES ISRAEL'S FIRST KING — BUT HE IS A FAILURE

1 KINGS

2 CHRONICLES

2 SAMUEL

1 CHRONICLES

ISRAEL (THE NORTH KINGDOM) IS EVENTUALLY EXILED IN ASSYRIA

2 KINGS

2 CHRONICLES

JUDAH (THE SOUTH KINGDOM) IS EVENTUALLY EXILED IN BABYLON

AFTER KING SOLOMON, THERE IS CIVIL WAR AND THE KINGDOM SPLITS

DAVID RULES AS KING OF ISRAEL

ESTHER NEHEMIAH EZRA

FROM ABOUT FIFTY YEARS LATER, THE EXILES OF JUDAH START TO COME HOME

The last group of exiles came home about 400 years before Christ

THROUGHOUT THIS TIME, ISRAEL HAD A SIMPLE (BUT DEMANDING) QUESTION TO ANSWER: <u>WHAT MAKES US SUCCESSFUL?</u>

THEY HAD TO LEARN THAT THESE ANSWERS WEREN'T RIGHT. INSTEAD, TO SURVIVE AS A NATION, THEY HAD TO KEEP FAITH WITH GOD...

When everyone is rich!

When the army is strong!

When our leaders are determined!

Make it your aim to do what is right, not what is evil, so that you may live. Then the Lord God Almighty really will be with you...

AMOS 5:14

37

JOSHUA

JOSHUA? WHO WAS HE?

JOSHUA HAD BEEN MOSES' RIGHT-HAND MAN SINCE THE TIME OF THE GREAT ESCAPE FROM EGYPT. HE WAS A BRILLIANT SOLDIER, AND BECAME LEADER OF ISRAEL AFTER MOSES HAD DIED.

AND WHAT'S THE BOOK ABOUT?

WELL, IT CHARTS THE CONQUEST OF CANAAN BY JOSHUA'S ARMY. THEY HAD TO DO BATTLE WITH THE PEOPLE WHO ALREADY LIVED THERE TO MAKE THEIR HOME.

River Jordan 4

THIS CONQUEST HAPPENED IN THREE PHASES...

1 THE FIRST STAB INTO CANAAN

AFTER SENDING IN SPIES TO GATHER INFORMATION, JOSHUA AND THE PEOPLE CROSS THE RIVER JORDAN INTO THE LAND GOD HAD PROMISED TO ABRAHAM CENTURIES BEFORE. THEY DEFEAT THE CITIES OF JERICHO AND AI. THIS GIVES THEM A SECURE BASE IN THE LAND (JOSHUA 1-8).

2 THE SOUTHERN CAMPAIGN

JOSHUA TURNS SOUTH AND WIPES OUT FIVE LOCAL KINGS. 'JOSHUA CONQUERED ALL THESE KINGS AND THEIR TERRITORY IN ONE CAMPAIGN BECAUSE THE LORD, ISRAEL'S GOD, WAS FIGHTING FOR ISRAEL' (JOSHUA 10:42). SEE JOSHUA 9-10 FOR THIS CAMPAIGN.

3 THE NORTHERN CAMPAIGN

A LARGE ARMY OF ISRAEL'S ENEMIES GATHERS IN THE NORTH. THEY'LL SHOW JOSHUA WHO'S IN CHARGE! BUT A SURPRISE ATTACK GIVES JOSHUA VICTORY. THE WAR IS OVER, BUT POCKETS OF THE LAND ARE STILL IN ENEMY HANDS. THIS CAUSES TROUBLE IN THE TIME OF THE JUDGES (JOSHUA 11).

THE REST OF THE BOOK LISTS THE LAND GIVEN TO EACH TRIBE OF ISRAEL. CHAPTERS 23 AND 24 GIVE JOSHUA'S FINAL SPEECH, AND THE AGREEMENT WITH GOD IS RENEWED.

JUDGES

IF YOU BUMPED INTO AN OLD TESTAMENT JUDGE IN THE STREET, HE (OR SHE) WOULD MORE LIKELY BE CARRYING A SWORD THAN WEARING A WIG! THE JUDGES WERE TWELVE MEN AND ONE WOMAN WHOM GOD CALLED TO RESCUE ISRAEL FROM ITS ENEMIES. THEY LIVED, FOUGHT AND DIED IN THE TROUBLED YEARS AFTER JOSHUA'S CONQUEST OF CANAAN.

JUDGES IS IN MANY WAYS A DEPRESSING BOOK. IT TELLS HOW THE PEOPLE OF ISRAEL REPEATEDLY REBELLED AGAINST GOD AND SET IN MOTION A GRIM CIRCLE OF EVENTS...

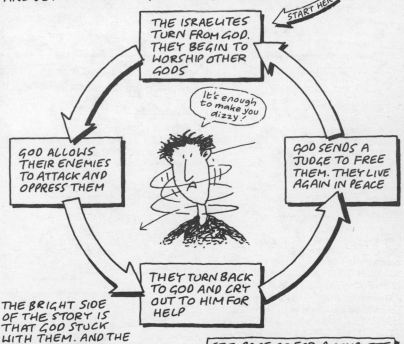

START HERE

THE ISRAELITES TURN FROM GOD. THEY BEGIN TO WORSHIP OTHER GODS

It's enough to make you dizzy!

GOD SENDS A JUDGE TO FREE THEM. THEY LIVE AGAIN IN PEACE

GOD ALLOWS THEIR ENEMIES TO ATTACK AND OPPRESS THEM

THEY TURN BACK TO GOD AND CRY OUT TO HIM FOR HELP

THE BRIGHT SIDE OF THE STORY IS THAT GOD STUCK WITH THEM. AND THE EXPLOITS OF THE JUDGES MAKES FOR INSPIRED READING.

SEE PAGE 40 FOR A COMPLETE LIST OF WHO ALL THE JUDGES HERE ...

DEBORAH

THE STORY OF DEBORAH IS TOLD IN JUDGES 4-5. SHE BECAME A NATIONAL HERO IN ISRAEL AT A TIME WHEN THE PEOPLE WERE SUFFERING UNDER THE VIOLENT RULE OF KING JABIN, AN INVADER FROM THE NORTH.

WHAT DID SHE DO?

SHE ROUSED THE NATION TO ACTION. AT HER COMMAND, A MILITARY LEADER CALLED BARAK GATHERED 10,000 MEN TO FIGHT KING JABIN.

WHO WERE THE JUDGES?

1 OTHNIEL JUDGES 3:7-11
2 EHUD JUDGES 3:12-30
3 SHAMGAR JUDGES 3:31
4 DEBORAH (WITH BARAK) JUDGES 4-5
5 GIDEON JUDGES 6-8
6 TOLA JUDGES 10:1-2
7 JAIR JUDGES 10:3-5
8 JEPHTHAH JUDGES 10:6 - 12:7
9 IBZAN JUDGES 12:8-10
10 ELON JUDGES 12:11-12
11 ABDON JUDGES 12:13-15
12 SAMSON JUDGES 13-16

BOXED NUMBERS ARE FOR JUDGES WITH MORE DETAILED, INTERESTING STORIES.

KING JABIN'S COMMANDER, SISERA, MASSED HIS 900 CHARIOTS AND MEN TO MEET THE ARMY OF ISRAEL. BARAK ATTACKED, AND IT SEEMS THAT THERE WAS ALSO A FLASH-FLOOD WHICH SWAMPED SISERA'S CHARIOTS. AND THEN... WELL, READ IT FOR YOURSELF! IT'S AN EPIC STORY, AND MANY OF THE DETAILS CAN BE FOUND IN DEBORAH'S SONG IN JUDGES CHAPTER 5.

The towns of Israel stood abandoned, Deborah; they stood empty until you came — came like a mother for Israel.

FROM THE SONG OF DEBORAH — JUDGES 5:7

SAMSON

SAMSON WAS THE LAST OF THE JUDGES, AND HE WAS LIKE A WILD-WEST MAVERICK: A GRITTY, GO-IT-ALONE, TRIGGER-HAPPY MOUNTAIN OF A MAN WITH MUSCLES IN PLACES WHERE MOST OF US DON'T EVEN HAVE PLACES. HE CARVED HIS WAY INTO THE BIBLE IN JUDGES CHAPTERS 13 TO 16.

> There are two things you need to know to understand Samson's story...

▷ DURING SAMSON'S LIFE, ISRAEL WAS OCCUPIED BY ITS OLD ENEMIES, THE PHILISTINES. ALTHOUGH SAMSON NEVER RALLIED AN ARMY TO DRIVE THEM OUT, HE WAGED A ONE-MAN WAR AGAINST THE PHILISTINES.

▷ SAMSON WAS RAISED AS A NAZARITE. THIS MEANT HE MADE PROMISES TO BE DEDICATED TO GOD IN A SPECIAL WAY. HE PROMISED NOT TO DRINK ALCOHOL, GO NEAR A DEAD BODY, OR CUT HIS HAIR. SAMSON BROKE ALL THESE PROMISES IN HIS LIFE, AND THIS LED TO HIS DOWNFALL.

AS A CHARACTER, SAMSON WAS LARGER THAN LIFE. IN BETWEEN HIS TRICKS OF TEARING DOWN CITY GATES BARE-HANDED AND TYING FLAMING TORCHES TO FOXES' TAILS, HE WAS ALSO A COMIC. AFTER KILLING SOME PHILISTINES WITH A DONKEY'S JAWBONE, HE SANG...

> With an ass's jaw I heaped them on the floor!

JUDGES 15:16

THIS GRIM MIXTURE OF SLAUGHTER AND COMEDY SUMS UP SAMSON'S WAYWARD LIFE.

> I tell you— he's a killer for jokes

see Judges 14:6

RUTH

A STORY FROM THE TIME OF JUDGES...

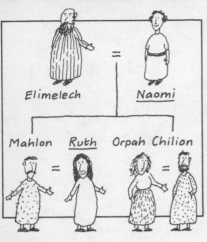

Elimelech = Naomi

Mahlon = Ruth   Orpah Chilion

How it all started

ELIMELECH TOOK HIS FAMILY FROM THEIR HOME IN BETHLEHEM TO LIVE IN MOAB (A FOREIGN COUNTRY). AFTER HE HAD DIED, HIS SONS MARRIED TWO LOCAL GIRLS. BUT TEN YEARS LATER, THE TWO SONS DIED AS WELL, AND NAOMI, THEIR MOTHER, DECIDED TO GO BACK HOME TO BETHLEHEM. RUTH, HER DAUGHTER-IN-LAW, INSISTED ON GOING BACK WITH HER, EVEN THOUGH SHE WOULD BE A FOREIGNER IN ISRAEL. HER LOYALTY TO HER MOTHER-IN-LAW, AND HER FAITH IN GOD ARE AMAZING...

The rest of the book

THE REST OF THE BOOK OF RUTH (FROM CHAPTER 2) IS THE LOVE STORY OF RUTH AND A RICH MAN CALLED BOAZ (WHO HAPPENED TO BE A RELATIVE OF NAOMI). THE STORY IS FULL OF ORIENTAL DETAILS AND IS A GREAT READ.

> Wherever you go, I will go... And your God will be my God.

RUTH TO NAOMI

THE BOOK HAS A SURPRISE ENDING IN RUTH 4:17. RUTH, IT TURNS OUT, IS GREAT-GRANDMOTHER TO NONE OTHER THAN KING DAVID.

FOREIGNERS

RUTH IS JUST ONE EXAMPLE OF NON-JEWS IN THE OLD TESTAMENT WHO WERE BLESSED BY GOD. IN LUKE 4:25-27, JESUS POINTED TO THE WIDOW OF ZAREPHATH (1 KINGS 17:8-24) AND NAAMAN (2 KINGS 5) AS OTHER SUCH FOREIGNERS. GOD'S LOVE WAS NOT STRICTLY CONFINED TO ONE NATION OR RACE, EVEN THEN.

◊   ◊   ◊

samuel

THIS PAGE FOCUSES ON SAMUEL, THE LEADER OF ISRAEL.

SAMUEL IS ONE OF THE GIANTS OF THE OLD TESTAMENT.

HE WAS LEADER OF GOD'S PEOPLE BETWEEN THE TIME OF THE JUDGES AND THE TIME OF THE KINGS.

HERE'S HIS PLACE AMONG THE OTHER GREATS OF THE OLD TESTAMENT...

ABRAHAM (Genesis)

JOSEPH (Genesis)

MOSES (Exodus–Deuteronomy)

SAMUEL (1 Samuel)

DAVID (1+2 Samuel)

ELIJAH (1 Kings)

ELISHA (2 Kings)

SAMUEL LED ISRAEL AT A TIME OF GREAT DANGER AND UNCERTAINTY. ISRAEL'S GREAT ENEMY, THE PHILISTINES (A WARLIKE RACE FROM THE COAST), WERE VERY POWERFUL. AND THE PEOPLE WERE OFTEN TEMPTED TO ABANDON GOD. SAMUEL WAS WHAT THEY NEEDED. HE WAS FAITHFUL TO GOD WHEN FEW OTHER PEOPLE WERE.

As Samuel grew up, the Lord was with him and made everything that Samuel said come true. So all the people of Israel, from one end of the country to the other, knew that Samuel was indeed a prophet of the Lord.

1 SAMUEL 3:19-20

KEY EVENTS

■ SAMUEL IS BORN – 1 SAMUEL 1

■ GOD SPEAKS TO YOUNG SAMUEL – 1 SAMUEL 3

■ SAMUEL BECOMES ISRAEL'S LEADER – 1 SAMUEL 4

■ SAMUEL THE RULER – 1 SAMUEL 7

■ SAMUEL AND KING SAUL – 1 SAMUEL 8-10

■ SAUL IS REJECTED AS ISRAEL'S KING – 1 SAMUEL 15

■ SAMUEL ANOINTS DAVID AS KING IN SECRET – 1 SAMUEL 16

■ SAMUEL DIES – 1 SAMUEL 25:1

1+2 Samuel

We'll take these two books in turn. First, I Samuel.

THE BOOK OF I SAMUEL FOLLOWS THE STORY OF ISRAEL AS THE NATION MOVED FROM RULE UNDER THE JUDGES TO RULE UNDER THE KINGS...

Judges ➤ Kings

BUT HOW DID ALL THIS HAPPEN?

THE PEOPLE OF ISRAEL WERE SICK OF BEING PUSHED AROUND BY THEIR OLD ENEMIES, THE PHILISTINES. THEY DECIDED THAT THE ANSWER WAS TO HAVE A KING...

THEY THOUGHT THEY WERE WEAK BECAUSE THEY DIDN'T HAVE A KING. BUT THE TRUTH WAS THAT THEY WERE WEAK BECAUSE THEY WERE YET AGAIN FAR FROM GOD.

We want a king!

Yeah! Like the other nations!

Someone to lead us in battle!

Someone who'll make us all rich!

Someone to go on the stamps!

(SEE I SAMUEL 8)

But just a minute! What was wrong with wanting a king anyway? Hadn't the judges been a bit like kings?

No, not really. The judges had been specially called by God to free Israel in times of crisis. Their leadership was in God's hands — He was their _real_ leader. But now the people wanted something different. They wanted a permanent series of rulers — kings whose sons would rule after them. God wouldn't have a say in calling leaders any more.

THIS WAS WHY GOD TOLD
SAMUEL (THE LEADER IN
ISRAEL AT THAT TIME – SEE
PAGE 43)...

> 66 You are not the one
> they have rejected;
> I am the one they have
> rejected as their king. 99
>
> I SAMUEL 8:7

DESPITE ALL THIS, GOD ALLOWED
HIS PEOPLE TO HAVE THEIR
KING. THE REST OF I SAMUEL
TELLS THE STORY OF SAUL
(THE FIRST KING) AND THE
STORY OF DAVID BEFORE HE
BECAME ISRAEL'S SECOND
KING. SEE PAGE 59 FOR MORE
ON DAVID.

THIS WAY

Ah! 2 Samuel!
I'd wondered
if you were
going to get
around to that
before this
page ended!

SAUL

FIRST KING OF ISRAEL. HE
APPEARS IN I SAMUEL 9-31.
SAUL FAILED TO DEFEAT
THE PHILISTINES ONCE AND
FOR ALL, AND HE FAILED
TO OBEY GOD. GOD
REJECTED HIM AS KING.
HE EVENTUALLY COMMITTED
SUICIDE.

DAVID

SECOND KING OF ISRAEL.
DAVID IS INTRODUCED IN
I SAMUEL 16 AND HIS STORY
CONTINUES THROUGH
2 SAMUEL TO END IN
I KINGS 2. DAVID WAS
ANOINTED SECRETLY IN
I SAMUEL 16 WHILE SAUL
WAS STILL RULING. HE
BECAME A NATIONAL HERO,
BUT SAUL HATED HIM AND
TRIED TO KILL HIM. DAVID
BECOMES KING AT THE
START OF 2 SAMUEL.

2 Samuel

2 SAMUEL SHOWS HOW THE MONARCHY FINALLY
GOT GOING IN ISRAEL. AFTER THE DISASTER
OF SAUL, EVERYONE HEAVED A SIGH OF
RELIEF THAT DAVID WAS ON THE THRONE.
HE DEFEATED ISRAEL'S ENEMIES (EVEN THE
PHILISTINES), EXPANDED HIS KINGDOM, AND
WAS POPULAR WITH EVERYONE. BUT FROM
2 SAMUEL 11 ONWARDS, DAVID AND HIS
KINGDOM WERE NEARLY DESTROYED THROUGH
HIS OWN STUPIDITY AND SIN. AT ONE POINT, HIS
OWN SON, ABSALOM, DECLARED WAR ON HIM...

Try reading
2 Samuel 9-20
and I Kings 1-2.
Read it in one
go, if you can.
It's a master-
piece of a
story...

THE FIRST BOOK OF

KINGS

THE BOOK OF 1 KINGS COVERS ABOUT 120 YEARS OF ISRAEL'S HISTORY. A LOT HAPPENED IN THAT TIME. AFTER DAVID CAME SOLOMON. AND AFTER SOLOMON THE KINGDOM WAS TORN IN TWO. FROM NOW ON, THERE WERE TWO KINGDOMS...

SOLOMON'S KINGDOM

NORTH KINGDOM: ISRAEL

SOUTH KINGDOM: JUDAH

ISRAEL
HAD AN UNSTABLE MONARCHY. KINGS WERE OVERTHROWN OR ASSASSINATED TO BE REPLACED BY OTHER KINGS. CAPITAL: SAMARIA.

JUDAH
WAS RULED IN A MORE STABLE WAY BY A SUCCESSION OF KING DAVID'S DESCENDANTS. CAPITAL: JERUSALEM.

1 KINGS TELLS THE STORY OF THIS SPLIT (WHICH WAS NEVER HEALED). THE BOOK CAN BE DIVIDED INTO THREE CHUNKS:

1 THE NEW KING

1 KINGS 1-2 RECORDS HOW SOLOMON BECAME KING AFTER THE DEATH OF KING DAVID.

2 SOLOMON

1 KINGS 3-11 FOCUSES ON THE REIGN OF KING SOLOMON. IT DESCRIBES IN GREAT DETAIL THE BUILDING OF THE TEMPLE IN JERUSALEM. THIS TEMPLE TOOK SEVEN YEARS TO BUILD. IT WAS TO BECOME THE FOCUS OF WORSHIP FOR THE JEWISH FAITH.

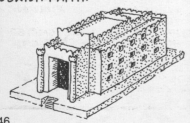

3 THE SPLIT

WHY DID IT HAPPEN?

THE KING AFTER SOLOMON WAS REHOBOAM. HE TOLD THE NORTH THAT HE WOULD RULE THEM WITH HARSHNESS. JEROBOAM LED THE NORTH INTO REBELLION AND BECAME THEIR KING (1 KINGS 11-12).

AND THEN..?

THE REST OF 1 KINGS TELLS THE STORY OF THE DIFFERENT KINGS, NORTH AND SOUTH. IT'S A DARK STORY, WHEN THE KINGS LED THE PEOPLE FAR FROM GOD. BUT GOD STILL WORKED THROUGH THE PROPHETS ELIJAH AND ELISHA...

SOLOMON

KING SOLOMON BECAME RULER OF ISRAEL AFTER DAVID, HIS FATHER, DIED. YOU CAN FIND HIM IN THE FIRST ELEVEN CHAPTERS OF 1 KINGS. HE IS STILL FAMOUS FOR THREE THINGS: HIS WISDOM, HIS WIVES, AND HIS WEALTH.

AT THE START OF HIS REIGN, SOLOMON ASKED GOD FOR WISDOM (1 KINGS 3). THIS PRAYER WAS ANSWERED GENEROUSLY! MANY OF THE PROVERBS THOUGHT UP BY SOLOMON ARE BELIEVED TO BE IN THE BOOK OF PROVERBS (SEE PAGE 62).

700 WIVES

TODAY WE MEASURE WEALTH BY THE SIZE OF YOUR HOUSE OR CAR. BUT IN SOLOMON'S TIME YOU KNEW IF SOMEONE WAS RICH IF HE COULD AFFORD TWO OR MORE WIVES. SOLOMON HAD 700. AND JUST TO MAKE SURE, HE ALSO HAD 300 WOMEN IN THE ROYAL HAREM.

NO DOUBT ABOUT IT— SOLOMON WAS <u>RICH</u>. HE'D INHERITED A STRONG, SECURE KINGDOM FROM KING DAVID (SEE PAGE 59), AND HE SPENT HIS LIFE MAKING IT FABULOUSLY WEALTHY. HE ALSO BECAME SOMETHING OF A WHEELER-DEALER INTERNATIONALLY. HIS FLEET OF SHIPS BROUGHT HOME EXOTIC GOODS LIKE GOLD, SPICES, IVORY, HORSES, APES AND PEACOCKS.

THIS WAY

Congratulations! I hear that you're seeing Solomon a year next October!

BUT...

SOLOMON'S REIGN WAS NOT THE GLITTERING SUCCESS IT SEEMED TO BE. BECAUSE:

- HE TAXED HIS PEOPLE HEAVILY TO PAY FOR HIS EXTRAVAGANCE
- HE USED FORCED WORKERS IN HIS AMBITIOUS BUILDING PROJECTS
- HIS FOREIGN WIVES TEMPTED HIM TO WORSHIP FOREIGN GODS

FOR THESE REASONS, KING SOLOMON HAS BEEN CALLED 'A WISE FOOL'.

SOLOMONIC 500 DOLLARS

AND CAN I PAY THE REST IN BABOONS?

That'll do nicely!

ELIJAH

ELIJAH. WHO WAS HE?

ELIJAH WAS A POWERFUL PROPHET IN THE NORTHERN KINGDOM OF ISRAEL. HE'S IN 1 KINGS 17 – 2 KINGS 2.

ER... JUST A MINUTE! WHAT DO YOU MEAN, A PROPHET?

WELL, AS A PROPHET, ELIJAH SPOKE OUT FOR GOD. HE WAS GOD'S MESSENGER, TELLING THE PEOPLE WHAT GOD WAS SAYING, AND HE WAS ALSO GOD'S AGENT, ACTING POWERFULLY FOR GOD. HE LIVED DURING A DARK PERIOD OF ISRAEL'S HISTORY, AROUND 100 YEARS AFTER KING DAVID. KING AHAB WAS ON THE THRONE, AND HIS MARRIAGE TO JEZEBEL (A FOREIGN PRINCESS WHO WAS LOYAL TO FALSE GODS) HAD SHOCKED ISRAEL.

👑 King Ahab 👑

ROYALLY COMMANDS YOU TO BE PRESENT AT HIS MARRIAGE TO

Princess Jezebel

DAUGHTER OF KING ETHBAAL OF SIDON

AT
THE ROYAL CAPITAL — SAMARIA

THE SERVICE WILL BE CONDUCTED BEFORE THE GODS OF SIDON AND ISRAEL

BRING YOUR OWN GODS   RSVP

JEZEBEL WAS DETERMINED TO MAKE HER GOD, BAAL, THE ONLY GOD OF ISRAEL. SHE WAS ELIJAH'S DEADLY ENEMY. THEIR FIGHT TOOK PLACE IN THREE ROUNDS...

1 THE 'GOD' BAAL WAS SUPPOSED TO BE BRILLIANT AT CONTROLLING THE WEATHER AND MAKING CROPS GROW. SO ELIJAH ANNOUNCED THAT GOD WAS SENDING A THREE-YEAR DROUGHT — AND IT HAPPENED. THIS SHOWED ISRAEL WHO WAS REALLY IN CONTROL OF THE WORLD. YOU CAN FIND THIS IN 1 KINGS 17.

FOR SALE

2 IN 1 KINGS 18, ELIJAH ARRANGED A DIRECT CONTEST BETWEEN HIMSELF AND THE 450 PROPHETS OF BAAL. IT'S ONE OF THE MOST DRAMATIC CHAPTERS OF THE OLD TESTAMENT. THE LORD WAS SHOWN TRULY TO BE GOD, THE PROPHETS OF BAAL WERE KILLED, AND ELIJAH HAD TO RUN FOR HIS LIFE FROM THE FURY OF QUEEN JEZEBEL.

3 1 KINGS 21. KING AHAB WANTED TO MAKE HIS GARDEN BIGGER. BUT HIS NEIGHBOUR, NABOTH, WOULDN'T SELL HIS LAND. JEZEBEL HAD HIM FRAMED, HE WAS STONED TO DEATH, AND AHAB GOT HIS GARDEN. FOR THIS, ELIJAH PRONOUNCED THE SENTENCE OF DEATH ON THEM BOTH. AHAB'S DEATH IS IN 1 KINGS 22, WHILE JEZEBEL'S IS IN 2 KINGS 9.

ELISHA

ELIJAH ➡ ELISHA

ELISHA WAS CALLED BY GOD AS A YOUNG MAN TO TAKE OVER FROM ELIJAH AS PROPHET TO ISRAEL. HE FIRST APPEARS IN I KINGS 19. IN 2 KINGS 2, AFTER THE DISAPPEARANCE OF ELIJAH, HIS PROPHETIC WORK STARTED. HE WAS TO BE A PROPHET FOR THE NEXT FIFTY YEARS.

Elisha ben Shaphat

Prophet, formerly Junior Partner to the late Elijah

PO BOX 77
NEAR SAMARIA
ISRAEL

Great Moments

AMONG THE GREAT MOMENTS IN ELISHA'S LIFE WERE...

- ◼ CALLED TO BE A PROPHET
  I KINGS 19:19-21
- ◼ SEES ELIJAH'S DEPARTURE
  2 KINGS 2
- ◼ ELISHA AND THE POOR
  WIDOW 2 KINGS 4:1-7
- ◼ ELISHA AND THE RICH
  WOMAN FROM SHUNEM
  2 KINGS 4:8-37
- ◼ HEALS NAAMAN, THE
  COMMANDER OF THE
  SYRIAN ARMY
  2 KINGS 5
- ◼ IN THE SIEGE OF SAMARIA,
  ELISHA PREDICTS ITS
  SUDDEN END
  2 KINGS 6:24-7:20

SO, WHICH OF THEM WAS GREATER — ELIJAH OR ELISHA?

WELL, ELISHA WAS REALLY THE JUNIOR PARTNER. HIS WORK AS A PROPHET WAS VERY MUCH LIKE SAMUEL'S.

AND WHAT ABOUT ELIJAH?

ELIJAH IS SEEN AS A CHARACTER WITH THE STATURE OF MOSES. AND THERE ARE MANY PARALLELS BETWEEN THE STORIES ABOUT THEM. (FOR EXAMPLE, ELIJAH MET WITH GOD ON MT SINAI, AND ELISHA SUCCEEDED ELIJAH IN EXACTLY THE SAME SORT OF WAY THAT JOSHUA SUCCEEDED MOSES.) BY THE TIME OF JESUS, MOSES REPRESENTED THE LAW, AND ELIJAH THE PROPHETS: THE TWO KEY FIGURES OF THE OLD TESTAMENT.

49

THE SECOND BOOK OF...

KINGS

2 KINGS CONTINUES THE STORY FROM WHERE 1 KINGS LEFT OFF. IT CHARTS THE DIRECTION ISRAEL AND JUDAH TOOK AS THEY HEADED ON A COLLISION COURSE WITH DISASTER. BECAUSE WITHIN 150 YEARS OF EACH OTHER, BOTH NATIONS HAD BEEN TAKEN VIOLENTLY INTO EXILE BY THE SUPERPOWERS OF THE TIME. 2 KINGS DOESN'T JUST TELL US ABOUT THESE DRAMATIC AND SHOCKING EVENTS — IT EXPLAINS WHY IT ALL HAPPENED. THE REAL REASON FOR THE DISASTER WAS THAT THE KINGS LED THEIR PEOPLE DEEPER AND DEEPER INTO SIN. AGAIN AND AGAIN THE WRITER OF 2 KINGS TELLS US —

HERE'S HOW THE BOOK WORKS...

1 STORIES ABOUT ELISHA
2 KINGS 1 – 8:15

2 KINGS OF JUDAH + ISRAEL
2 KINGS 8:16 – 17:4

3 SAMARIA IS SMASHED AND ISRAEL IS TAKEN INTO EXILE
2 KINGS 17:5-41

4 THE KINGDOM OF JUDAH
2 KINGS 18-24

5 JERUSALEM FALLS, JUDAH GOES INTO EXILE
2 KINGS 25

> He, like the kings before him, sinned against the Lord...

What were these sins? Come on! Out with them!

- FOLLOWED FALSE GODS AND GODDESSES
- SACRIFICED YOUNG CHILDREN TO PAGAN GODS
- RICH PEOPLE OPPRESSED THE POOR (SEE PAGES 80-81)

2 KINGS 17:7-18 GIVES THE REASONS IN FULL.

How it Happened

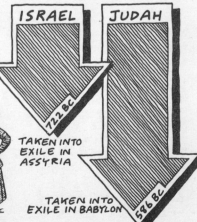

ISRAEL

JUDAH

722 BC

TAKEN INTO EXILE IN ASSYRIA

586 BC

TAKEN INTO EXILE IN BABYLON

1+2 CHRONICLES

Right! Let's get one thing straight from the start. These books of Chronicles — they're just repeating the stuff in 2 Samuel and Kings, aren't they? Go on, admit it!

CHRONICLES IS DIFFERENT FROM 2 SAMUEL AND KINGS BECAUSE OF WHAT IT OMITS AND FOR WHAT IT ADDS...

OMITS IT LEAVES OUT DAVID'S PERSONAL LIFE (BATHSHEBA, ABSALOM, ETC.), AND MOST OF THE STORY OF THE NORTHERN KINGDOM.

No they aren't! They're quite different. Now get your foot off my leg!

ADDS IT ADDS A LOT OF MATERIAL ABOUT THE TEMPLE AND THE RELIGIOUS SIDE OF ISRAEL'S LIFE. WHOEVER WROTE CHRONICLES SELECTED CAREFULLY WHAT HE WANTED TO INCLUDE.

But why did he do it?

The skeleton of the books...

BECAUSE HE WANTED TO SPOTLIGHT TWO THINGS THAT GOD HAD BROUGHT INTO BEING:

1 THE LINE OF KINGS DESCENDED FROM DAVID

2 THE TEMPLE IN JERUSALEM

FAMILY TREES 1 CHRON. 1-9

KING SAUL DIES 1 CHRON. 10

KING DAVID'S ACHIEVEMENTS
1 CHRON. 11-29

KING SOLOMON'S RULE
2 CHRON. 1-9

THE NORTH-SOUTH SPLIT
2 CHRON. 10

THE KINGS OF JUDAH
2 CHRON. 11-36:12

JERUSALEM FALLS!
2 CHRON. 36:13-23

IT'S RECKONED THAT THESE BOOKS WERE WRITTEN FOR THE EXILES OF JUDAH WHO RETURNED HOME FROM BABYLON YEARS LATER. THEY NEEDED TO BE ENCOURAGED THAT THEY WERE STILL PART OF DAVID'S KINGDOM, AND THAT THE TEMPLE AND ITS WORSHIP WERE STILL IMPORTANT. (FOR MORE ON THE EXILE, SEE PAGES 74-75).

EZRA

IF YOU'VE JUST READ 1 AND 2 CHRONICLES, YOU COULD BE IN FOR A PLEASANT SURPRISE — EZRA CONTINUES THE STORY. SO JUST CARRY ON READING! IN FACT, THE BOOKS OF CHRONICLES, EZRA AND NEHEMIAH MAKE UP A FOUR-VOLUME SET. SO IT'S GOOD TO TRY TO READ THEM TOGETHER.

NOW YOU'VE BOUGHT THOSE, WHY NOT READ THESE TOO?

So what is the book all about?

THE PEOPLE OF JUDAH WERE DRAGGED OFF INTO EXILE IN 586 BC. THEY WERE HELD CAPTIVE IN THE MIGHTY EMPIRE OF BABYLON. BUT NEARLY FIFTY YEARS LATER, BABYLON WAS OVER-THROWN BY KING CYRUS OF PERSIA. CYRUS WAS A MORE HUMANE RULER, AND HE ENCOURAGED ALL BABYLON'S EXILES TO RETURN HOME. EZRA SHOWS THE RETURN TO JERUSALEM OF SOME OF THE EXILES.

THE BOOK CAN BE DIVIDED INTO THREE PARTS...

1 <u>EZRA 1-2</u> KING CYRUS ORDERS THE JEWISH EXILES TO RETURN AND REBUILD THE TEMPLE

2 <u>EZRA 3-6</u> SLOWLY, THE TEMPLE IS REBUILT AND WORSHIP BEGINS AGAIN (SEE THE BOOKS OF HAGGAI AND ZECHARIAH FOR MORE DETAILS)

3 <u>EZRA 7-10</u> EZRA COMES TO JERUSALEM. MIXED MARRIAGES ARE ENDED

EZRA

EZRA IS A KEY FIGURE AT THIS POINT IN THE BIBLE'S STORY. IN EXILE, THE JEWISH PEOPLE LOST EVERYTHING THAT HELD THEM TOGETHER: THEIR KING, TEMPLE AND CITY. BUT THEY FOUND A NEW NATIONAL FOCUS IN THE LAW OF MOSES AND ITS RELIGIOUS PRACTICES SUCH AS THE SABBATH AND CIRCUMCISION. BY LAYING DOWN THE LAW IN THE WAY HE DID, EZRA HELD THE JEWISH PEOPLE TOGETHER.

NEHEMIAH

THIS BOOK FOLLOWS THE STORY OF NEHEMIAH. HE LED A GROUP OF EXILES HOME TO JERUSALEM AND REBUILT THE CITY'S RUINED WALLS. WHEN WE FIRST MEET HIM IN NEHEMIAH CHAPTER 1, HE IS THE KING'S WINE-TASTER. LIKE ESTHER AND DANIEL (SEE PAGES 54 + 76), HE HAD REACHED A VERY HIGH POSITION IN THE ROYAL COURT. HE RECEIVED THE KING'S PERMISSION TO REBUILD JERUSALEM, AND HE WAS MADE GOVERNOR. ALL THIS IS IN NEHEMIAH 1-2.

AS THE KING'S WINE-TASTER NEHEMIAH PROBABLY LOOKED LIKE THIS...

SABOTAGE!

NEHEMIAH 3-7 MAKES VERY EXCITING READING! NEHEMIAH'S ENEMIES STARTED BY MOCKING THE WALL-BUILDERS:

> Can you make building stones out of heaps of burned rubble?

> Even a fox could knock it down!

BUT THE MOCKERY SOON TURNED INTO THREATS, ATTACKS, PLOTS ON NEHEMIAH'S LIFE, AND FALSE REPORTS TO THE KING. NEHEMIAH SUCCEEDED BECAUSE OF HIS FAITH IN GOD...

> But now, God, make me strong!

NEHEMIAH'S PRAYER

> In Nehemiah 8-10, Ezra appears and reads the 'Book of the Law' (probably the Bible's first five books) to the people. Shocked that they have disobeyed God's law, they turn back to him.

> In the last chapters (11-13) Nehemiah leads a joyful procession around the newly-completed walls of Jerusalem. Against all the odds, the Jewish people had returned home in style.

ESTHER

THE BOOK OF ESTHER, LIKE THE BOOKS OF EZEKIEL AND DANIEL, IS SET IN THE TIME OF THE JEWISH EXILE. IT TELLS THE STORY OF A JEWISH WOMAN CALLED ESTHER, WHO MARRIED THE PERSIAN KING AND SAVED HER PEOPLE FROM BEING EXTERMINATED BY THEIR ENEMIES. THERE ARE FOUR MAIN CHARACTERS IN THE STORY...

KING XERXES (ALSO KNOWN AS AHASUERUS IN SOME VERSIONS). HE HAD POWERS OF LIFE AND DEATH OVER ALL HIS SUBJECTS.

QUEEN ESTHER, XERXES' NEW WIFE. BY HER COURAGE AND QUICK-WITTEDNESS SHE AVERTED DISASTER.

HAMAN, THE PRIME MINISTER. AFTER MORDECAI HAD INSULTED HIM, HE PLANNED TO HAVE ALL THE JEWS IN THE PERSIAN EMPIRE KILLED.

MORDECAI, COUSIN TO ESTHER. WORKING WITH ESTHER, HE TURNED HAMAN'S THREAT INTO A JEWISH TRIUMPH.

NOW READ IT FOR YOURSELF! →

POETRY + WISDOM

THIS SECTION
CONTAINS THE BOOKS OF...

JOB, PSALMS,
PROVERBS, ECCLESIASTES
AND THE SONG OF SONGS

Poetry + Wisdom

IN THIS SECTION WE LOOK AT FIVE BOOKS — JOB, PSALMS, PROVERBS, ECCLESIASTES AND THE SONG OF SONGS. THREE OF THEM (JOB, PROVERBS AND ECCLESIASTES) ARE WHAT IS KNOWN AS 'WISDOM BOOKS'. AND ALL OF THEM USE POETRY. SO LET'S LOOK AT POETRY FIRST...

POETRY

THE HEBREW PEOPLE WERE A SINGING PEOPLE. AT SEVERAL POINTS THE OLD TESTAMENT BREAKS INTO SONG (SEE MOSES' SONG IN EXODUS 15, DAVID'S LAMENT IN 2 SAMUEL 1, ETC.). IT SEEMS THAT THEIR SINGING WAS FAMOUS INTERNATIONALLY (PSALM 137:3). THE MOST FAMOUS BOOK OF JEWISH POETRY, THE PSALMS, IS ACTUALLY A SONG BOOK.

ALL RIGHT! ALL RIGHT! DON'T HARP ON ABOUT IT!

THIS WAY

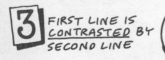

HEBREW POETRY IS DIFFERENT FROM POETRY AS WE KNOW IT — IT DOESN'T USE RHYME, FOR INSTANCE. INSTEAD, IT RELIES ON SPECIAL METHODS OF REPEATING IDEAS. HERE ARE THREE WAYS THESE ANCIENT POETS DID IT...

1 FIRST LINE IS REPHRASED IN SECOND LINE

I am gripped by fear and trembling;
I am overcome with horror.

PSALM 55:5

2 FIRST LINE IS AMPLIFIED BY SECOND LINE

I wish I had wings, like a dove.
I would fly away and find rest.

PSALM 55:6

3 FIRST LINE IS CONTRASTED BY SECOND LINE

His words were as smooth as oil,
But they cut like sharp swords.

PSALM 55:21

THE PSALMS (AND OTHER BITS OF BIBLICAL POETRY) ARE BURSTING WITH IMAGES AND EXTRAVAGANT, POETIC LANGUAGE. IN THESE POEMS, TREES CLAP THEIR HANDS, HILLS SING FOR JOY, GOD'S ENEMIES MELT LIKE WAX, THE SUN IS LIKE A SPRINTER, GOD RIDES ON THE CLOUDS, AND HIS LAW IS SWEETER THAN HONEY. WHEN WE'RE READING THESE BOOKS IT'S WISE TO REMEMBER THAT WE'RE LOOKING AT <u>POETRY</u>.

WISDOM

THE WISDOM BOOKS OF THE BIBLE WEREN'T WRITTEN BY OUT-OF-TOUCH PHILOSOPHERS LIVING IN RENTED IVORY TOWERS. THESE BOOKS ARE ABOUT <u>REAL LIFE</u>!

THEY COME IN TWO VARIETIES

THE BIBLE'S WISDOM IS TARGETTED ON THE HEART — IN OTHER WORDS, WHERE WE MAKE ALL OUR MORAL AND MENTAL DECISIONS.

1

PROVERBIAL

THE BOOK OF PROVERBS FALLS INTO THIS CATEGORY. IT CONTAINS BRILLIANTLY-WRITTEN, TWO-LINE SAYINGS THAT GIVE SOLID ADVICE FOR EVERYDAY LIFE.

2

INVESTIGATIVE

JOB AND ECCLESIASTES ARE IN THIS CATEGORY. JOB USES DIALOGUE AND ECCLESIASTES USES MONOLOGUE TO INVESTIGATE THE REAL MEANING OF LIFE.

THE WISDOM WRITERS WANTED THEIR READERS TO REMEMBER THEIR PROVERBS. SO THEY USED MEMORY-AIDS IN WRITING THEM:

■ IN PROVERBS 30:15, ETC., THERE ARE SOME SAYINGS USING NUMBERS — 'THERE ARE FOUR THINGS...'

■ PROVERBS 31:10-31 IS A POEM. THE FIRST LETTER OF EACH NEW VERSE STARTS WITH THE NEXT LETTER OF THE HEBREW ALPHABET.

■ MANY PROVERBS USE COMEDY. ONCE YOU'VE READ AND LAUGHED AT THEM, THEY STICK IN YOUR MIND!

JOB

IF YOU'VE EVER ASKED YOURSELF 'WHY DO GOOD PEOPLE SUFFER?' THEN JOB IS FOR YOU...

WHAT'S IT ALL ABOUT?

THE BOOK TELLS THE STORY OF A MAN CALLED JOB (RHYMES WITH <u>ROBE</u>). HE WAS A GOOD MAN, FAITHFUL TO GOD, AND MUCH LOVED BY HIS FAMILY AND FRIENDS.

SO WHAT HAPPENED TO HIM?

JOB WAS STRUCK DOWN BY A SERIES OF DISASTERS. HIS ANIMALS WERE STOLEN, LIGHTNING COOKED ALL HIS SHEEP AND SHEPHERDS, A DESERT STORM KILLED HIS KIDS, AND FINALLY HE WAS COVERED FROM HEAD TO FOOT WITH AN EPIC CASE OF BOILS. ALL THIS HAPPENS BY CHAPTER 2!

HOW DOES THE STORY WORK OUT?

It's enough to make you sick!

THIS WAY

IN CHAPTERS 3-37 JOB ASKS 'HOW CAN GOD ALLOW THIS TO HAPPEN TO ME?' THREE FRIENDS, ELIPHAZ, BILDAD AND ZOPHAR, ATTEMPT TO ANSWER HIM. THEIR MAIN ARGUMENT IS THAT JOB <u>MUST</u> HAVE DONE SOMETHING TERRIBLY WRONG TO HAVE DESERVED SO MUCH SUFFERING. BUT JOB KNOWS HE HAS NOT WRONGED GOD IN THIS WAY, AND BECOMES MORE AND MORE ANGRY AT HIM. JOB ENDS BY LONGING FOR GOD TO SPEAK UP AND ANSWER ALL HIS QUESTIONS...

GOD REPLIES

GOD 'ANSWERS' JOB IN CHAPTERS 38 – 41. HE SPEAKS OUT OF A STORM AND GIVES A GLORIOUS DEMONSTRATION OF HIS POWER. HE SEEMS TO BE SAYING: 'TRUST ME. I KNOW WHAT I'M DOING!' JOB'S GOOD FORTUNES ARE THEN RESTORED TO HIM.

David

KING DAVID RANKS AS ONE OF THE BEST-KNOWN AND BEST-LOVED KINGS IN HISTORY. HE RULED ANCIENT ISRAEL BETWEEN THE YEARS 1010 AND 970 BC. BUT HE WAS MUCH MORE THAN JUST ANOTHER KING, AS THESE JOB DESCRIPTIONS SHOW...

1 Shepherd

AS A YOUNG BOY, DAVID WAS IN CHARGE OF HIS FATHER'S SHEEP. BUT THIS WAS NO 'SOFT' JOB — HE HAD TO FIGHT OFF WILD ANIMALS WHO FANCIED A QUICK LEG OF LAMB (SEE 1 SAMUEL 17:34-37).

Saved our bacon, he did!

2 Poet

DAVID IS FAMOUS AS A WRITER OF PSALMS AND POEMS. MANY OF THE PSALMS, TRADITIONALLY CREDITED TO DAVID, REFLECT HIS EXPERIENCES:

- PSALM 23 — THE SHEPHERD
- PSALMS 54, 57 — WHEN DAVID WAS BEING HUNTED BY KING SAUL
- PSALM 18 — DAVID GIVES THANKS FOR ESCAPING FROM SAUL AND OTHERS
- PSALM 3 — DAVID ON THE RUN FROM HIS SON, ABSALOM
- PSALM 51 — DAVID'S SONG OF REPENTANCE AFTER HIS ADULTERY WITH BATHSHEBA

(SEE PAGES 45 AND 46 FOR DETAILS ON THESE EVENTS.)

4 King

DAVID'S EARLY LIFE IS TOLD IN THE BOOK OF 1 SAMUEL. HE BECOMES KING AT THE START OF 2 SAMUEL. DAVID RULED OVER A GOLDEN AGE IN ISRAEL, AND HE WAS LATER SEEN AS A LEGENDARY FIGURE, THE IDEAL RULER FOR GOD'S PEOPLE. HERE ARE SOME OF HIS KEY EVENTS...

- BECOMES KING, CAPTURES JERUSALEM (2 SAMUEL 1+5)
- BRINGS THE ARK TO JERUSALEM (2 SAMUEL 6)
- COMMITS ADULTERY AND MURDER (2 SAMUEL 11-12)
- ABSALOM REBELS AGAINST DAVID (2 SAMUEL 13-19)

3 Soldier

DAVID HAD TO WAIT MANY YEARS BEFORE HE BECAME ISRAEL'S KING — AND HE SPENT THESE YEARS AS A BRILLIANT SOLDIER. HIS CAREER BEGAN WITH HIS DEFEAT OF THE GIANT GOLIATH (1 SAMUEL 17).

PSALMS

THE BOOK OF PSALMS IS THE LONGEST BOOK IN THE BIBLE, AND IT'S ALSO ONE OF THE BIBLE'S HIGH POINTS. IT CONTAINS 150 'PSALMS' (POEMS OR SONGS). IT HAS BEEN USED AS <u>THE</u> HYMN BOOK AND PRAYER BOOK BY JEWS AND CHRISTIANS ALIKE. AS WE READ THEM, WE NEED TO REMEMBER THAT THE PSALMS ARE POEMS OR LYRICS.

Play it again, Psalm!

So how were the psalms used?

SOME OF THE PSALMS WERE PERSONAL, PRIVATE PRAYERS. BUT MANY WERE CLEARLY WRITTEN FOR WORSHIP OR PRAYER <u>TOGETHER</u>. IN THE TIMES OF THE OLD TESTAMENT, THIS WAS DONE IN THE TEMPLE IN JERUSALEM.

And what was this worship like?

IN A WORD, <u>NOISY</u>! SOME OF THE PSALMS ARE QUIET AND REFLECTIVE, BUT ON THE WHOLE THE BOOK IS FULL OF SHOUTING AND DANCING, AND PSALM 150 THROWS IN TRUMPETS, DRUMS, HARPS, FLUTES AND CYMBALS – <u>LOUD</u> CYMBALS. PSALM 71:22-23 AND PSALM 81:1-2 GIVE PICTURES OF WHAT THIS WORSHIP WAS LIKE.

MAX. 22 DECIBELS

IN THE NEW TESTAMENT, JESUS QUOTES A LOT FROM THE PSALMS (SOME OF HIS LAST WORDS ARE FROM PSALM 22). THE FIRST CHRISTIANS ALSO KNEW THE PSALMS BACKWARDS (SEE PETER'S SERMON IN ACTS 2). CHRISTIANS HAVE ALWAYS VALUED THE PSALMS MORE THAN ANY OTHER OLD TESTAMENT BOOK...

The Book of Psalms could well be called a 'little Bible' since it contains, set out in the briefest and most beautiful form, all that is to be found in the whole Bible.

MARTIN LUTHER

IN THE PSALMS, THE WRITERS EXPRESS THE FULL MENU OF HUMAN EMOTIONS BEFORE GOD. THIS IS ONE OF THEIR GREAT STRENGTHS. THEY SHOW US PEOPLE BEING REAL WITH GOD. THE PSALMS EXPRESS...

...ANGER
Wake up, Lord! Why are you asleep? Rouse yourself! Don't reject us for ever!
PSALM 44

...WORSHIP
Sing to the Lord, all the world! Worship the Lord with joy!
PSALM 100

...LONGING
From the depths of my despair I call to you, Lord.
PSALM 130

...TRUST
You, Lord, are all I have, and you give me all I need; my future is in your hands.
PSALM 16

Then there's joy, loneliness, thankfulness, peace, repentance and so on... Try to read them for yourself.

A TASTER

IF YOU FEEL A BIT DAUNTED BY THE THOUGHT OF WADING THROUGH ALL 150 PSALMS, TRY READING THIS 'TOP TWENTY' SELECTION, WHICH INCLUDES SOME OF THE BEST KNOWN. TICK OFF THE BOXES AS YOU READ EACH PSALM.

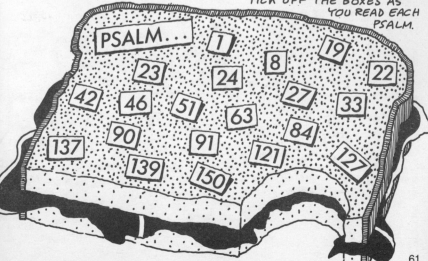

PSALM... 1 8 19 23 24 22 42 46 51 27 33 90 63 84 137 91 121 127 139 150

61

PROVERBS

YOU'VE GOTTA KISS A LOTTA FROGS BEFORE YOU MEET THE HANDSOME PRINCE

AMERICAN PROVERB

THE EARLY BIRD CATCHES THE WORM

TRADITIONAL ENGLISH PROVERB

SIC FREAT CRUSTULUM (THAT'S THE WAY THE COOKIE CRUMBLES)

COOKED-UP LATIN PROVERB

IF YOU LIKE HEARING OR COLLECTING PROVERBS, THEN YOU HAVE AT LEAST ONE THING IN COMMON WITH SOME OF THE ANCIENT ISRAELITES. THEIR 'WISE MEN' LOVED TO COLLECT AND POLISH UP PROVERBS. THE BOOK OF PROVERBS CONTAINS A FEW SUCH COLLECTIONS.

SO, IN A WORD, EXACTLY <u>WHAT IS</u> THIS BOOK OF PROVERBS?

IT'S A GUIDE TO SUCCESSFUL LIVING. IF YOU WANT TO BE WISE, IT GIVES LOTS OF PRACTICAL, HARD-HEADED ADVICE ON WHAT TO DO IN DIFFERENT SITUATIONS.

AND IT'S WRITTEN BY KING SOLOMON?

MANY OF THE PROVERBS ARE CREDITED TO SOLOMON, WHO IS STILL FAMOUS FOR HIS WISDOM. YOU CAN FIND THESE ASSORTED PROVERBS FROM CHAPTER 10 ONWARDS.

Here are a few proverbs to get you started...

Let other people praise you — even strangers; never do it yourself

Without wood, a fire goes out. Without gossip, quarrelling stops.

A fool doing some stupid thing a second time is like a dog going back to its own vomit.

'THE WISE MAN' IS PRAISED IN PROVERBS

'THE FOOL' IS A FIGURE OFTEN CRITICIZED IN PROVERBS

Now <u>where</u> did I put it?

ECCLESIASTES

ECCLESI–WHAT?

ECCLESIASTES. THE BOOK CONTAINS THE WORDS OF 'THE PHILOSOPHER' OR 'THE PREACHER' AS HE CALLS HIMSELF. BUT BASICALLY IT'S ABOUT THE MEANING OF LIFE, THE UNIVERSE AND EVERYTHING.

THE BOOK STARTS OFF ON A LOW NOTE–

IT IS USELESS, USELESS, SAID THE PHILOSOPHER. LIFE IS USELESS, ALL USELESS. YOU SPEND YOUR LIFE WORKING, AND WHAT DO YOU HAVE TO SHOW FOR IT?

AND THEN IT GETS WORSE. IF THE BOOK OF PROVERBS IS GENERALLY OPTIMISTIC ABOUT LIFE, THEN ECCLESIASTES IS GENERALLY PESSIMISTIC.

The Search

THE PHILOSOPHER TRIES TO FIND HAPPINESS AND MEANING IN LAUGHTER, ENJOYMENT, RICHES AND SUCCESS, WISDOM AND RELIGION. BUT THEY ALL FAIL. IN THE END, DEATH MAKES THEM ALL MEANINGLESS. AND EVEN GOD SEEMS UNJUST AND UNPREDICTABLE – 'YOU NEVER KNOW WHAT KIND OF BAD LUCK YOU ARE GOING TO HAVE IN THIS WORLD...'

SO WHY IS SUCH A NEGATIVE, DESPAIRING BOOK IN THE BIBLE AT ALL?

WELL...

■ THE BOOK SHOWS US THAT IT'S NO GOOD IGNORING THE DARK SIDE OF LIFE, HOPING IT WILL JUST GO AWAY. IT WON'T! WE HAVE TO FACE UP TO IT HONESTLY, AS THE PHILOSOPHER DOES.

■ WE NEED TO READ THE BOOK AS ONE SMALL PART OF THE WHOLE BIBLE. THE PHILOSOPHER DOESN'T FIND ANSWERS, BUT OTHER PARTS OF THE BIBLE CAN HELP US WITH OUR DIFFICULT QUESTIONS.

AAAAARGH!

Song of Songs

THIS SMALL BOOK IS ONE OF THE MOST BEAUTIFUL IN THE BIBLE. IT'S CALLED 'THE SONG OF SONGS' MEANING THAT IT'S THE BEST OF ALL SONGS. IN SOME VERSIONS OF THE BIBLE IT'S CALLED 'THE SONG OF SOLOMON'.

Please tell us about it. Please, Please!

OKAY.

IT IS SPRING, APPROPRIATELY ENOUGH. IN DAZZLINGLY BEAUTIFUL COUNTRYSIDE, WHILE THE FLOWERS GROW AND THE FOXES RUN, TWO YOUNG LOVERS CELEBRATE THEIR LOVE IN A SERIES OF SONGS. THE SONGS ARE INTENSELY PASSIONATE, WITH RICH PHYSICAL AND SEXUAL IMAGERY. THEY CAPTURE THE FULL EXPERIENCE OF HUMAN LOVE.

THE SONG OF SONGS IS VERY MUCH AN EASTERN BOOK. WARNING: SQUEAMISH WESTERNERS MIGHT FIND SOME OF THE DESCRIPTIONS TOO EXPLICIT! AND THEN SOME OF THE IMAGES ARE DELIGHTFULLY FOREIGN TO US.

Her neck... is like a tower

His eyes... are like doves washed in milk

IT'S ALL VERY ROMANTIC. ALL IT LACKS IS A SUNSET...

YES, YES, YES — BUT WHAT'S A LOVE SONG DOING IN THE BIBLE?

TO SHOW THE HIGH VALUE THAT GOD PUTS ON HUMAN LOVE. TO SHOW (AS ONE WRITER PUT IT) THAT 'GOD THOUGHT OF SEX FIRST'.

Place me like a seal
   over your heart,
like a seal over your arm;
for love is as strong as
   death,
its jealousy unyielding
   as the grave.
It burns like blazing fire,
like a mighty flame.
Many waters cannot
   quench love;
rivers cannot wash it
   away.

The conclusion (Song of Songs 8:6-7)

THE PROPHETS

THIS SECTION CONTAINS THE BOOKS OF...

ISAIAH, JEREMIAH, LAMENTATIONS, EZEKIEL, DANIEL, HOSEA, JOEL, AMOS, OBADIAH, JONAH, MICAH, NAHUM, HABAKKUK, ZEPHANIAH, HAGGAI, ZECHARIAH AND MALACHI

PHEW!

THE PROPHETS

THE SECTION OF THE BIBLE BETWEEN ISAIAH AND MALACHI (WHICH ENDS THE OLD TESTAMENT) IS KNOWN AS 'THE PROPHETS'. IT RECORDS THE LIVES AND MESSAGES OF GOD'S COURAGEOUS MESSENGERS TO ISRAEL AND JUDAH.

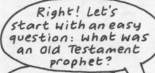

Right! Let's start with an easy question: what was an Old Testament prophet?

That's simple! Someone who predicted the future.

Wrong!

THE PROPHETS DID TALK ABOUT THE FUTURE, BUT IT WASN'T THEIR MAIN JOB. THEY WERE CALLED BY GOD TO SPEAK HIS MESSAGES TO ISRAEL AND JUDAH, WHEN BOTH NATIONS HAD TURNED AWAY FROM HIM. THEY ATTACKED THE WORSHIP OF OTHER GODS. THEY BLAZED WITH ANGER WHEN THE RICH CHEATED AND TROD ON THE POOR. THEY TOLD THEM **EXACTLY** WHAT GOD THOUGHT OF THEM. NATURALLY, THEY WEREN'T TOO POPULAR...

You WANT ME TO SAY **THAT**?

To THEM?

BUT HOW DID THE PROPHETS KNOW WHAT MESSAGE TO GIVE? THEY KNEW BECAUSE THEY WERE SO CLOSE TO GOD. THIS IS WHY THEY COULD SAY SO CONFIDENTLY —

THE LORD, WHO MADE THE EARTH, SPOKE TO ME...

JEREMIAH

THE LORD SAYS TO THE PEOPLE OF ISRAEL, 'COME TO ME AND YOU WILL LIVE.'

AMOS

66

So where does predicting the future come in?

Well, the prophets warned God's people that if they didn't mend their ways, then disaster would strike in the future. And after disaster HAD struck and the people were in exile, the prophets promised that God would bring them home again in the future. These things came true. It's important to see that when the prophets talked about tomorrow, it wasn't just to satisfy people's curiosity (like newspaper horoscopes) but to show them how to live TODAY.

The prophets were treated badly because few people liked what they had to say. Here's a taste of their experience...

They will defy and despise you; it will be like living among scorpions.

GOD CALLS EZEKIEL (2:6)

This man must be put to death!

A PLOT AGAINST JEREMIAH (38:4)

Jerusalem, Jerusalem! You kill the prophets, you stone the messengers God has sent you!

JESUS IN LUKE 13:34

Was there ANY prophet that your ancestors did not persecute?

STEPHEN IN ACTS 7:52

If you want to know when the prophets spoke, this chart will help you.

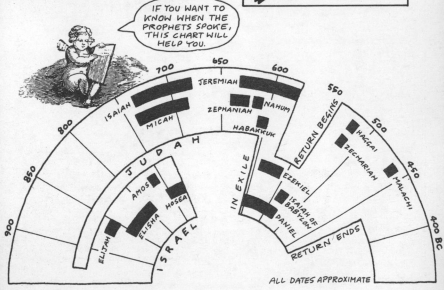

ALL DATES APPROXIMATE

ISAIAH

ISAIAH – WHO WAS HE?

<u>NAME</u> ISAIAH, SON OF AMOZ

<u>OCCUPATION</u> PROPHET TO JUDAH

<u>CAREER</u> CALLED TO BE A PROPHET IN THE YEAR KING UZZIAH DIED (SEE ISAIAH 6). PROPHESIED IN JERUSALEM FOR FORTY YEARS

<u>OTHER INFO</u> REPUTED TO BE OF ROYAL BLOOD. POSSIBLY KILLED BY KING MANASSEH

THE ISAIAH FILE

But did Isaiah the Prophet write Isaiah the Book?

THAT'S NOT SUCH A STUPID QUESTION AS IT LOOKS! HERE'S THE PROBLEM...

CHAPTERS 1-39 CONTAIN PROPHECIES GIVEN <u>BEFORE</u> JUDAH WENT INTO EXILE.

CHAPTERS 40-66 DESCRIBE IN DETAIL EVENTS AT THE <u>END</u> OF THE EXILE, 150 YEARS LATER.

ISAIAH 1-39

ISAIAH 40-55
ISAIAH 56-66

SOME PEOPLE BELIEVE GOD ENABLED ISAIAH SON OF AMOZ TO SEE INTO THE FUTURE IN THIS DETAILED WAY. OTHERS THINK IT'S MORE LIKELY THAT CHAPTERS 40-66 WERE THE WORK OF ISAIAH'S LATER DISCIPLES, WRITING AT THE END OF THE EXILE. IF THIS SECOND OPTION IS CORRECT, IT'S IMPORTANT TO REMEMBER THAT THESE CHAPTERS CAME FROM PEOPLE WHO CLOSELY FOLLOWED ISAIAH'S TEACHING. THE WHOLE BOOK THEREFORE HAS A UNITY OF THOUGHT, IF NOT A UNITY OF AUTHORSHIP.

> Whatever happened, the Book of Isaiah is powerful, with many themes that are worth investigating.

GLOOM & DOOM

IN PART ONE (ISAIAH 1–39), ISAIAH ATTACKS THE SITUATION IN JUDAH BEFORE THE EXILE. JERUSALEM HAD BECOME A WEALTHY CITY, AND THE RICH WERE RIPPING OFF THE POOR AND HELPLESS. ALSO, BECAUSE OF THE THREAT OF FOREIGN INVASION, JUDAH HAD MADE A NUMBER OF TREATIES WITH NATIONS THAT FOLLOWED FALSE GODS. ISAIAH SAID THAT GOD WAS ANGRY WITH ALL THIS AND WOULD PUNISH HIS PEOPLE FOR BREAKING FAITH WITH HIM.

> You are doomed! You will be carried away as prisoners. Your leaders will starve to death and the common people will die of thirst.
>
> ISAIAH 5

HOPE & GLORY

> Jerusalem, be strong and great again! Holy city of God, clothe yourself with splendour! The heathen will never enter your gates again.
>
> ISAIAH 52

IN PART TWO (FROM ISAIAH 40), THE MESSAGE CHANGES DRAMATICALLY TO GIVE HOPE AND COMFORT FOR THE EXILES OF JUDAH IN BABYLON. AFTER THE END OF CHAPTER 55, THE PROPHET GIVES MESSAGES OF WARNING TO THE RETURNED EXILES. ONE THEME IN ALL THESE CHAPTERS IS THAT GOD CONTROLS ALL THAT GOES ON IN THE WORLD (SEE ISAIAH 40 ESPECIALLY).

Two of the most famous chapters in the book are Isaiah 53 and 61. Isaiah 53 points forward in detail to the death of Jesus Christ, over 500 years later. And Isaiah 61 was quoted by Jesus in Luke 4:16–30 at the start of his work.

jeremiah

THE PROPHETS AS A GROUP HAD A PRETTY THIN TIME OF IT. THEIR MESSAGES ABOUT GOD'S JUDGMENT WERE UNPOPULAR AND UNWANTED. BUT IF YOU HAVE TO CHOOSE TO BE AN OLD TESTAMENT PROPHET, THEN DON'T CHOOSE JEREMIAH! HE HAD THE WORST TIME OF THE LOT.

If you're trying to get our sympathy, <u>forget</u> it! Jeremiah was a traitor - he was just plain unpatriotic!

traitor!

THAT'S EXACTLY HOW JEREMIAH WAS SEEN IN HIS TIME. HE HAD TO TELL THE PEOPLE OF JUDAH THAT GOD WAS GOING TO PUNISH THEIR SINS. HE HAD TO TELL THEM THAT THE MIGHTY BABYLONIANS WOULD DESTROY THEIR NATION AND SMASH JERUSALEM, THE CITY THEY LOVED. AND WHEN THE BABYLONIANS DID ATTACK, WHILE EVERYONE ELSE WAS TRYING TO KEEP MORALE UP, JEREMIAH TOLD THEM TO GIVE IN AND ACCEPT GOD'S JUDGMENT. HE WAS BEATEN, IMPRISONED, THROWN INTO A MUDDY CISTERN, THREATENED WITH DEATH, AND SO ON. IT WASN'T PLEASANT.

Poor Jeremiah! I wonder how he felt about it all...

WELL, HE DIDN'T ENJOY IT. SOMETIMES THINGS GOT SO BAD THAT HE MOANED TO GOD, BUT IT WAS NO USE...

When I say, 'I will forget the Lord and no longer speak in his name,' then your message is like a fire burning deep within me. I try my best to hold it in, but can no longer keep it back.

JEREMIAH 20:9

70

So how long was Jeremiah a prophet for?

Forty years — and he saw his worst prophecies fulfilled. The Book of Jeremiah records his amazing life and message, but not in the order that events happened.

HERE ARE TWO WAYS TO LOOK AT THIS GREAT BOOK...

1 His Message

JEREMIAH HAD AN URGENT MESSAGE TO PUT ACROSS. SO HE OFTEN USED PICTURES AND DRAMATIC ACTIONS TO DRIVE HIS WORDS HOME. TRY LOOKING AT SOME OF THESE: THE ALMOND BRANCH AND THE BOILING POT (CHAPTER 1). THE POTTER AT WORK (CHAPTER 18). THE SMASHED POT (CHAPTER 19). GOOD FIGS AND BAD FIGS (CHAPTER 24). THE WOODEN AND IRON YOKES (CHAPTERS 27 + 28). JEREMIAH'S ENEMIES MAY HAVE HATED HIS WORDS, BUT THEY COULDN'T FORGET THEM!

AT TIMES, JEREMIAH SAW AND HEARD THE FUTURE SO VIVIDLY THAT HE WAS TERRIFIED. JEREMIAH 4:13, 19-22 IS A GOOD EXAMPLE OF THIS.

ALTHOUGH JEREMIAH HAD A TOUGH MESSAGE TO PREACH, WHEN THE DISASTERS HE HAD PREDICTED STARTED TO HAPPEN, HE BEGAN TO SPEAK ABOUT HOPE FOR THE FUTURE. GOD'S PUNISHMENT WOULDN'T LAST FOR EVER. IN THE GREATEST PASSAGE OF THE BOOK (JEREMIAH 31:31-34) HE LOOKS FORWARD TO A NEW AGREEMENT WITH GOD, WHICH WILL CHANGE PEOPLE FROM THE INSIDE. THIS AGREEMENT WAS ONLY FULFILLED WITH THE COMING OF JESUS CHRIST.

2 His Life

HERE ARE SOME OF THE MAIN EVENTS IN JEREMIAH'S LIFE:

- JEREMIAH 1 CALLED TO BE A PROPHET BY GOD.
- JEREMIAH 26 ARRESTED!
- JEREMIAH 32 THE SIEGE OF JERUSALEM BEGINS. JEREMIAH BUYS A FIELD.
- JEREMIAH 37 IN THE SIEGE, HE IS IMPRISONED.
- JEREMIAH 38 HE IS FLUNG INTO A MUDDY CISTERN, AND LEFT TO DIE.
- JEREMIAH 39 JERUSALEM FALLS TO THE BABYLONIANS.
- JEREMIAH 40-43 HE IS TAKEN BY FORCE TO EGYPT.

Lamentations

The Book of Lamentations is a collection of five poems (one per chapter) mourning the destruction of Jerusalem by the Babylonian army. The poems were probably written very soon after the fall of the city. The person who wrote them almost certainly was an eyewitness to all the terrible suffering.

SO WHAT DO THESE POEMS **SAY**?

1 THEY WEEP OVER THE DESTRUCTION

THE POEMS USE SHORT SENTENCES IN A KIND OF SOBBING RHYTHM TO LAMENT OVER THE RUINED CITY. THE DESTRUCTION IS DESCRIBED IN VIVID DETAIL, AND THE ENEMIES MOCK: 'IS THIS THAT LOVELY CITY? IS THIS THE PRIDE OF THE WORLD?' (LAMENTATIONS 2:15).

2 THEY ADMIT THE PEOPLE'S GUILT

THE POEMS INSIST THAT ALL THIS MISERY IS NOT SOME ACCIDENT OR TWIST OF FATE. INSTEAD, IT IS ONLY THE JUST PUNISHMENT THAT GOD HAD WARNED WOULD HAPPEN: 'WE HAVE SINNED AND REBELLED, AND YOU, O LORD, HAVE NOT FORGIVEN US' (LAMENTATIONS 3:42). GOD HAS GIVEN HIS ANGER FULL EXPRESSION.

3 THEY PUT THEIR HOPE IN GOD

DESPITE THE WEEPING AND ANGUISH THAT FILLS THIS BOOK, THERE IS **SOME** HOPE. INCREDIBLY, DESPITE ALL THE VIOLENCE AND KILLING, THE WRITER IS ABLE TO LOOK TO GOD: 'THE LORD'S UNFAILING LOVE AND MERCY STILL CONTINUE...' (LAMENTATIONS 3:22). THE BOOK CLOSES WITH THIS PRAYER...

Bring us back to you, Lord! Bring us back!
Restore our ancient glory.
Or have you rejected us forever?
Is there no limit to your anger?

LAMENTATIONS 5:21-22

EZEKIEL

FORTY-EIGHT CHAPTERS! A BIT LONG, ISN'T IT?

LET ME EXPLAIN. EZEKIEL WAS CALLED AS PROPHET TO A GROUP OF EXILES LIVING IN BABYLONIA. THIS GROUP HAD BEEN EXILED BEFORE THE FALL OF JERUSALEM, AND SO THE FIRST PART OF THE BOOK CONTAINS PROPHECIES GIVEN BEFORE THAT ALL HAPPENED.

CHAPTERS 1-32
MESSAGES OF WARNING AND JUDGMENT

JERUSALEM FALLS 586 BC

CHAPTERS 33-48
MESSAGES OF HOPE

EZEKIEL'S MESSAGE CHANGED TO ONE OF HOPE AFTER THE FALL OF JERUSALEM. THIS WAS BECAUSE THE EXILES WERE IN TOTAL DESPAIR AT THE LOSS OF THEIR HERITAGE. THEY ASKED QUESTIONS LIKE...

WHERE WAS GOD WHEN JERUSALEM WAS DESTROYED?

THERE'S NO HOPE FOR US NOW- IS THERE?

THE GODS OF BABYLON MUST BE MORE POWERFUL THAN OUR GOD. THEY DEFEATED HIM!

KEY PASSAGES

EZEKIEL 1-3 GOD CALLS EZEKIEL TO BE A PROPHET

EZEKIEL 4 EZEKIEL ACTS OUT THE SIEGE OF JERUSALEM

EZEKIEL 34 THE SHEPHERDS OF ISRAEL

EZEKIEL 36:16-38 THE PROMISE OF NEW LIFE

EZEKIEL 37 THE VALLEY OF DRY BONES

EZEKIEL TACKLED THESE PROBLEMS IN THIS WAY...

- LIKE THE OTHER PROPHETS, HE SHOWED THE EXILE WAS BECAUSE OF JUDAH'S SINS.
- HE SAID THERE WAS HOPE BECAUSE GOD WOULD BRING THE EXILES HOME.
- HE GAVE A VISION OF GOD AS THE SOVEREIGN LORD, POWERFUL AND TRANSCENDENT.

THE EXILE

In 597BC, disaster fell upon Judah. Babylon, the superpower of that time, overran the country and took all the leading citizens into exile in Babylonia, 800 miles from home. The Jewish people, who had once been slaves in Egypt, were now slaves once again.

THE EXILE HAPPENED IN THREE STAGES...

1 IN 604 BC, KING JEHOIAKIM AND OTHER CAPTIVES WERE LED INTO EXILE.

2 IN 597 BC, KING JEHOIACHIN AND OTHERS WENT INTO EXILE IN BABYLON.

3 IN 586 BC, THE SAME THING HAPPENED TO KING ZEDEKIAH. THIS TIME, JERUSALEM WAS TOTALLY DESTROYED.

Why did it happen?

FOR ALL SORTS OF REASONS. HERE'S HOW SOME OF THE PEOPLE MIGHT HAVE PUT IT...

Because the nation was corrupt! The rich made slaves of the poor, and leaders misled the people...

ISAIAH

Because God's people refused to keep God's laws.

EZEKIEL

Because Judah would not give up the worship of false gods!

JEREMIAH

Because the King of Judah was rebelling against my rule. I needed to teach him a lesson!

NEBUCHADNEZZAR, EMPEROR OF BABYLON

EACH OF THESE REASONS CONTAINED A PIECE OF THE TRUTH. TAKEN TOGETHER, THEY ADDED UP TO THE GUILTY VERDICT FOR JUDAH.

Behind all these reasons, the prophets saw the hand of God. It was God, they said, who was punishing them for all of their sins.

Oh, I see...
But how did they *live* in exile?

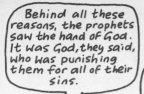

WELL, JEREMIAH THE PROPHET WROTE TO ONE OF THE FIRST GROUPS OF EXILES (SEE JEREMIAH 29) TELLING THEM HOW TO SETTLE DOWN. THIS IS PROBABLY HOW THEY LIVED IN EXILE —

Build houses and settle down. Plant gardens and eat what you grow in them. Marry and have children. Then let your children get married, so that they also may have children. You must increase in numbers and not decrease. Work for the good of the cities where I have made you go as prisoners. Pray to me on their behalf, because if they are prosperous, you will be prosperous too.
— P.T.O.

JEREMIAH (SPEAKING ON GOD'S BEHALF) SAID THE EXILE WOULD LAST SEVENTY YEARS. THEN GOD WOULD BRING THEM HOME.

BUT EVEN FOR THOSE EXILES WHO LIVED PROSPEROUSLY IN BABYLON (AND MANY DIDN'T) THERE WAS DESPAIR. NOTHING COULD TAKE AWAY THE PAIN OF LOSING THE LAND THAT THEY LOVED...

How can we sing a song to the Lord in a foreign land?
May I never be able to play the harp again if I forget you, Jerusalem!

PSALM 137:4-5

THEN, AS JEREMIAH HAD PREDICTED, THE EXILE CAME TO AN END. THE CRUEL BABYLONIAN EMPIRE WAS CONQUERED BY THE MORE TOLERANT PERSIANS, WHO ALLOWED EXILED PEOPLES TO GO HOME.

ASSYRIA   BABYLON   PERSIA

BABYLON CONQUERS ASSYRIA 612 BC

PERSIA CONQUERS BABYLON 539 BC

DANIEL

You know, I've been thinking about this Book of Daniel. It seems to me that it's more like <u>two</u> books than one...

<u>Two</u>? Waddaya mean?

Well, chapters 1-6 tell the adventures of Daniel and his friends, who were a group of young Jewish exiles, training in the royal court of Babylon.

But chapters 7-12 are totally different! They record a series of strange visions Daniel had, predicting the future.

Part One

IN THESE CHAPTERS (DANIEL 1-6), YOUNG DANIEL RISES QUICKLY TO A KEY POSITION IN THE ROYAL COURT AT BABYLON. HE WAS THERE FOR NEARLY SEVENTY YEARS — THROUGHOUT THE WHOLE JEWISH EXILE. LIKE JOSEPH (IN GENESIS 41), DANIEL BECAME SUCCESSFUL BY INTERPRETING THE KING'S DREAMS. AND LIKE JOSEPH, HE PUBLICLY SAID THAT IT WAS GOD, NOT HIMSELF, WHO PROVIDED THE MEANING.

THE DANIEL STORIES AREN'T JUST ENTERTAINMENT. THEY WERE WRITTEN TO ENCOURAGE JEWISH PEOPLE FACING HARD TIMES UNDER HARSH, FOREIGN RULERS WHO WANTED THEM TO GIVE UP THEIR FAITH. THESE CHAPTERS IN DANIEL TELL THEM, IN EFFECT...

- STICK BY THE JEWISH FOOD LAWS! (DANIEL 1)
- DON'T GIVE IN AND WORSHIP FALSE GODS! (DANIEL 3)
- DON'T ABANDON YOUR RELIGIOUS LIFE! (DANIEL 6)

Grrrr! I could eat half a dozen Daniels for <u>breakfast</u>!

(HOWEVER, SEE DANIEL 6)

76

Part Two

Part 2 of Daniel is very different from Part 1. But the thing they have in common is that they were both written to inspire Jewish people in tough times. Part 2 does this through a sequence of visions that show God is in control of history.

HOWEVER, BE WARNED! THESE VISIONS ARE <u>WEIRD</u>. IF YOU THINK YOU SUFFER FROM STRANGE DREAMS, TRY READING DANIEL 7-12! DANIEL IS DIFFERENT FROM ALL THE OTHER OLD TESTAMENT PROPHETS IN GIVING US THESE NIGHTMARISH VISIONS THAT ARE FULL OF COMPLICATED SYMBOLISM...

Vision 1

DANIEL SEES FOUR STRANGE BEASTS, REPRESENTING FOUR EMPIRES. THEY ARE JUDGED BY GOD, WHO GIVES POWER TO A GLORIOUS 'SON OF MAN'.
<u>DANIEL 7</u>

Vision 2

DANIEL SEES A GOAT DEFEAT A RAM. THE GOAT (REPRESENTING A GREAT EMPIRE) HAS FOUR HORNS. ONE OF THESE GROWS A LITTLE HORN THAT CAUSES HAVOC FOR GOD'S PEOPLE.
<u>DANIEL 8</u>

Vision 3

A GLORIOUS FIGURE APPEARS TO DANIEL AND GIVES A DETAILED PREDICTION OF THE FUTURE.
<u>DANIEL 10-12</u>

Fine! But what does it all mean?

THE VISIONS MOSTLY GIVE A BLOW-BY-BLOW ACCOUNT OF THE HISTORY OF THE TIME. BUT THEY ALSO POINT FORWARD TO THE END OF TIME, WHEN GOD WILL REVEAL HIS GREAT POWER (SEE DANIEL 7:9-14 AND DANIEL 12). THE ONLY OTHER BOOKS IN THE BIBLE TO USE VISIONS LIKE THESE ARE ZECHARIAH, PARTS OF EZEKIEL, AND REVELATION.

H♥SEA

THIS IS THE STORY OF A BROKEN MARRIAGE. HOSEA AND A WOMAN CALLED GOMER MARRIED AND HAD THREE CHILDREN. BUT THEN GOMER WAS UNFAITHFUL AND WENT TO LIVE WITH HER LOVERS. EVEN THOUGH SHE BECAME A PROSTITUTE, HOSEA STILL LOVED HER AND BOUGHT HER BACK TO BE HIS WIFE AGAIN (HOSEA 1-3).

THROUGH THIS TRAGEDY IN HIS OWN LIFE, HOSEA SAW DEEPLY HOW GOD FELT ABOUT ISRAEL'S UNFAITHFULNESS TO HIM. HOSEA'S MARRIAGE BECAME A PICTURE OF GOD'S MARRIAGE TO HIS PEOPLE.

Israel, I will make you my wife;
I will be true and faithful...

GOD SPEAKING IN HOSEA 2:19

Hosea was prophet to the northern kingdom of Israel about the same time Isaiah was in the south. His message was harsh — because of the people's sins, Israel would be swallowed up by war.

So there was no hope, then?

SURPRISINGLY, THERE WAS HOPE IN HOSEA'S MESSAGE. JUST AS HOSEA TOOK HIS WIFE BACK, SO GOD COULD NEVER FORGET HIS PEOPLE. THE BOOK'S MOST HOPEFUL WORDS ARE...

How can I give you up, Israel?
How can I abandon you?
My heart will not let me do it!
My love for you is too strong.

HOSEA 11:8

JOEL

THE PROPHET JOEL PROBABLY LIVED SOME TIME BETWEEN 500 AND 300 BC, WHEN THE JEWISH PEOPLE WERE SETTLED IN THEIR LAND AGAIN AFTER THE EXILE WAS OVER. JOEL'S BOOK BEGINS WITH A TERRIBLE PLAGUE OF LOCUSTS THAT HAD TURNED THE LAND INTO A DESERT.

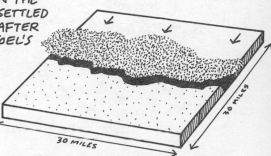

30 MILES

30 MILES

DIARY OF A LOCUST

born! eat. eat.
eat, eat, eat,
eat, eat, munch,
eat.

TO BE CONTINUED...

DID YOU KNOW? LOCUSTS EAT ALL THE VEGETATION ON LAND. AN AVERAGE SWARM DEVOURS 900 SQUARE MILES PER DAY!

Judgment!

HOWEVER, JOEL WASN'T JUST A 'REPORTER ON THE LOCUST DISASTER. HE SAW THE LOCUSTS AS A PICTURE OF WHAT GOD'S JUDGMENT WOULD BE LIKE AT THE END OF HISTORY. LIKE THE LOCUSTS, GOD'S JUDGMENT WOULD BE...

- A DAY OF DARKNESS
- THE DESTRUCTION OF ALL THOSE THINGS REGARDED AS GOD'S BLESSINGS — CROPS, VINES, ETC.
- UNSTOPPABLE. YOU CAN'T SWAT A SWARM OF LOCUSTS — YOU CAN'T STOP GOD'S WRATH.

SEE JOEL 1 AND 2.

THIS VISION OF JUDGMENT, SAID JOEL, SHOULD MAKE US TURN BACK TO GOD. THEN HE WILL RESTORE ALL THE GOOD THINGS WE HAVE LOST BECAUSE OF OUR SIN (JOEL 2: 12 -27). BUT THEN JOEL LOOKS FURTHER AHEAD IN TIME (JOEL 2: 28-32) TO WHEN GOD WILL GIVE HIS SPIRIT TO ALL PEOPLE. THESE WORDS ARE SAID TO HAVE COME TRUE IN ACTS 2: 14-36.

66 I will pour out my Spirit on all people. Your sons and daughters will prophesy, your old men will dream dreams, your young men will see visions. **99**

JOEL 2:28

AMOS

AMOS WAS JUST A QUIET SHEPHERD FROM JUDAH — UNTIL GOD CALLED HIM. HE WAS TOLD TO LEAVE HIS SHEEP, TRAVEL NORTH TO ISRAEL, AND PREACH A VERY TOUGH, DANGEROUS MESSAGE TO THE PEOPLE THERE. ALTHOUGH HIS BOOK IS QUITE SHORT, AMOS WAS ONE OF THE GREATEST OLD TESTAMENT PROPHETS. HE PROPHESIED AROUND 760 BC.

So what was his message all about?

To understand Amos, we first have to go back in time a bit...

...TO **Moses**

IN THE TIME OF MOSES, GOD DELIVERED THE ISRAELITES FROM SLAVERY IN EGYPT (SEE PAGE 28). MOSES TOLD THEM THAT IF THEY WERE FAITHFUL TO GOD, THEY WOULD NEVER BE SLAVES AGAIN. THIS MEANT THAT THEY WERE <u>ALL EQUAL</u>. EACH PERSON WAS TO HAVE HIS OWN PIECE OF THE PROMISED LAND, WHICH HIS FAMILY WOULD HOLD FOR EVER. NO ONE COULD BUY OR STEAL IT FROM THEM. BUT BY AMOS'S TIME, THESE GOD-GIVEN VALUES HAD BROKEN DOWN.

ON THE SURFACE, EVERYTHING SEEMED FINE. ISRAEL, UNDER THE RULE OF KING JEROBOAM II, WAS ENJOYING A RARE PERIOD OF PEACE AND PLENTY. TRADE WAS UP. THE SHEKEL WAS DOING WELL. MANSIONS WERE BEING BUILT. EVEN RELIGION WAS BOOMING. BUT AS AMOS POINTED OUT, THESE GOOD TIMES WERE ONLY FOR THE WEALTHY FEW. MANY PEOPLE IN ISRAEL LIVED IN SUFFOCATING POVERTY.

And <u>what</u>, if I may ask, was wrong with <u>that</u>?

EVERYTHING WAS WRONG WITH IT!
AS IN MOST COUNTRIES THROUGHOUT
HISTORY, THE RICH KEPT THEM-
SELVES RICH AND POWERFUL BY
MAKING SURE THE POOR STAYED
POOR AND WEAK. IF YOU HAD
STOOD ON ANY STREET CORNER
IN ISRAEL IN AMOS'S TIME, YOU
MIGHT HAVE HEARD THE RICH
SAYING...

So you can't afford to pay me for those sandals I let you have last week? Right! You'll have to let me sell you as a slave — or else I'll have you thrown in prison!

Excuse me, Judge, please accept this small 'gift'. I do hope you will turn down that miserable beggar who's accusing me in court today...

See that poor man over there? He owes me bags of money. I'll pay you two very well if you beat him up and bring any valuables in his house to me...

WHAT MADE IT EVEN WORSE,
SAID AMOS, WAS THAT THE RICH
WERE OUTWARDLY VERY RELIGIOUS. THEY EVEN THOUGHT THEY
WERE RICH BECAUSE GOD HAD BLESSED THEM. BUT WHAT THEY
WERE DOING TO THE POOR VIOLATED ALL MOSES HAD TAUGHT.

WHEAT
50
FINEST QUALITY

66 LISTEN TO THIS, YOU THAT
TRAMPLE ON THE NEEDY AND
TRY TO DESTROY THE POOR OF
THE COUNTRY. YOU SAY TO
YOURSELVES, 'WE CAN HARDLY
WAIT FOR THE HOLY DAYS TO BE
OVER SO THAT WE CAN SELL OUR
CORN... THEN WE CAN OVER-
CHARGE, USE FALSE MEASURES,
AND TAMPER WITH THE SCALES
TO CHEAT OUR CUSTOMERS. WE
CAN SELL WORTHLESS WHEAT
AT A HIGH PRICE. 99 AMOS 8:4-6

AMOS THUNDERED AGAINST
THE RICH IN ISRAEL FOR
ALL THESE SINS. HIS
MESSAGE WAS CLEAR: THE
ALL-POWERFUL GOD LOVED
THE POOR AND WEAK, AND HE
SAW WHAT WAS HAPPENING
TO THEM. IF ISRAEL DID NOT

LEARN TO GIVE THEM JUSTICE,
THEN DESTRUCTION WOULD
CERTAINLY COME.

LESS THAN FORTY YEARS
LATER, THE ASSTRIAN ARMY
INVADED, TAKING ALL THE
RICH PEOPLE INTO EXILE...

Obadiah

OBADIAH IS THE SHORTEST BOOK IN THE OLD TESTAMENT. THERE AREN'T EVEN ANY CHAPTERS — ONLY VERSES. IN THIS SHORT, VIVID POEM, OBADIAH PROPHESIES THE DOWNFALL OF EDOM, A KINGDOM TO THE SOUTH OF JUDAH.

> WHY DID HE DO THAT?

> WELL, IT'S A LONG STORY!

BAD BLOOD

ISRAEL AND EDOM WENT BACK A LONG WAY. RIGHT BACK TO JACOB AND HIS BROTHER ESAU IN GENESIS. ISRAEL WAS DESCENDED FROM JACOB, EDOM FROM ESAU. ALTHOUGH RELATED, THE TWO NATIONS CONSTANTLY FEUDED THROUGHOUT THE OLD TESTAMENT. SAUL FOUGHT THEM, DAVID CONQUERED THEM, BUT THEY CONTINUED TO BE A PAIN IN JUDAH'S SIDE, INVADING OR REBELLING WITH MONOTONOUS REGULARITY.

THEN IN 586 BC CAME THE FINAL BLOW: BABYLON ATTACKED AND DESTROYED JERUSALEM. INSTEAD OF HELPING THEIR BROTHERS, THE EDOMITES ENCOURAGED THE BABYLONIANS. THEY HANDED OVER ESCAPING JUDEANS, LOOTED THE FALLEN CITY, AND GLOATED OVER THE WHOLE DISASTER. PSALM 137 REMEMBERS HOW THE EDOMITES HAD URGED ON JERUSALEM'S DESTRUCTION:

> Tear it down to the ground!
>
> PSALM 137:7

OBADIAH PRONOUNCED DOOM ON EDOM FOR THIS TREACHERY. THE EDOMITES THOUGHT THEY WERE UNBEATABLE. THEIR KINGDOM WAS ON TOP OF A MOUNTAIN APPROACHED THROUGH A NARROW CANYON — THE PERFECT DEFENSE! BUT OBADIAH SAID THEY WOULD BE UTTERLY DEFEATED. IN THIS WAY, GOD WOULD JUDGE THEM FOR THEIR LACK OF HUMANITY TOWARDS A BROTHER-NATION IN THEIR HOUR OF EXTREME NEED.

> AND DID IT HAPPEN AS OBADIAH SAID?

YES. BY THE FIFTH CENTURY BC, EDOM HAD FALLEN TO ARAB INVADERS.

THE BOOK OF JONAH IS COMPLETELY DIFFERENT FROM THE OTHER BOOKS OF THE PROPHETS. IT TELLS THE STORY OF JONAH, A RELUCTANT PROPHET WHO TRIED HARD TO DISOBEY GOD — BUT FAILED!

GOD TOLD JONAH...

GO TO NINEVEH!

GOD WANTED THE PEOPLE OF NINEVEH (THE ASSYRIAN CAPITAL) TO TURN FROM THEIR EVIL WAYS. BUT JONAH WOULDN'T GO TO DELIVER GOD'S MESSAGE. LIKE OTHER PEOPLE OF HIS TIME, JONAH HATED THE ASSYRIANS. HE KNEW THAT GOD WAS SENDING HIM TO GIVE THEM THE CHANCE TO REPENT AND BE FORGIVEN. JONAH WOULD HAVE PREFERRED THEM TO BE DESTROYED. SO HE HEADED OFF IN THE OPPOSITE DIRECTION. BUT GOD OVERRODE JONAH'S PLANS. JONAH ENDED UP IN THE STOMACH OF A GREAT FISH WHICH WAS HEADING — YOU GUESSED IT — IN THE DIRECTION OF NINEVEH.

MUST HAVE BEEN MY BIG BROTHER. HE'D EAT _ANYTHING_.

THE STORY ENDS WITH JONAH AT NINEVEH. THE CITY REPENTS AND ITS PEOPLE ARE FORGIVEN BY GOD. JONAH IS FURIOUS AND GOD HAS TO REBUKE HIM FOR HIS COLD-HEARTEDNESS. THE WHOLE POINT OF THE BOOK (LIKE THE BOOK OF RUTH, SEE PAGE 42) IS THAT GOD IS CONCERNED FOR _ALL_ PEOPLE, NOT JUST THE PEOPLE OF ISRAEL (JONAH 4: 10-11).

Did it Really Happen?

YES!

SOME PEOPLE BELIEVE THE EVENTS IN JONAH ARE HISTORICAL.

OTHERS THINK JONAH IS A PARABLE. LIKE JESUS' PARABLE OF THE GOOD SAMARITAN, IT ISN'T HISTORICAL, THEY SAY, BUT IT HAS IMPORTANT THINGS TO TEACH.

NO!

EITHER WAY, JONAH TELLS US A LOT ABOUT GOD.

micah

MICAH THE PROPHET WAS ONE OF THE FOUR GREAT PROPHETS WHO SPOKE OUT DURING THE 8TH CENTURY BC. THEY WERE —

AMOS & HOSEA

PROPHESIED IN NORTHERN KINGDOM OF ISRAEL

ISAIAH & MICAH

PROPHESIED IN SOUTHERN KINGDOM OF JUDAH

Micah spoke at a time when Judah and Israel were as bad as the pagan nations next door. These nations followed false gods, who were thought to bring rain, good harvests and success in battle when they were given the right amount of animal (and human) sacrifices and religious ritual. Judah and Israel thought this was how it was with God. As long as they kept up their religious duties, they would placate God and could live as they liked.

MICAH SPOKE OUT AGAINST THIS STRONGLY. HIS GREAT THEME WAS THAT GOD IS A GOD OF JUSTICE — AND HE EXPECTED HIS PEOPLE TO SHOW JUSTICE IN THE WAY THEY TREATED EACH OTHER. HE DIDN'T WANT THOUSANDS OF ANIMAL SACRIFICES. HE DIDN'T WANT MECHANICAL, EMPTY WORSHIP. INSTEAD...

66 WHAT DOES THE LORD REQUIRE OF YOU?
TO ACT JUSTLY AND TO LOVE MERCY
AND TO WALK HUMBLY WITH YOUR GOD. 99
MICAH 6:8

HOPE!

LIKE AMOS, HOSEA AND ISAIAH, MICAH PRONOUNCED THE GUILTY VERDICT ON GOD'S PEOPLE. BUT HE ALSO SAW SIGNS OF HOPE IN TWO PLACES...

JERUSALEM
IN MICAH 4:1-5, JERUSALEM BECOMES THE RELIGIOUS FOCUS FOR THE WORLD. THIS FAMOUS PASSAGE TALKS ABOUT PEACE AND GOD'S BLESSING COMING FROM ISRAEL.

BETHLEHEM
IN MICAH 5:2-4, A RULER TO BRING HOPE TO THE WHOLE WORLD IS PROMISED. SEE MATTHEW 2:6.

NAHUM AND HABAKKUK

THE TIME IS CLOSE TO THE YEAR 600 BC. NAHUM AND HABAKKUK, TWO PROPHETS, WERE BOTH CONCERNED ABOUT THE WAY THAT JUDAH WAS AT THE MERCY OF THE MIGHTY SUPERPOWERS OF THAT TROUBLED TIME. THE ASSYRIAN EMPIRE, WHICH HAD CRUELLY TREATED JUDAH FOR YEARS, WAS ABOUT TO BE VIOLENTLY OVERTHROWN BY THE BABYLONIANS.

NAHUM

NAHUM IS A TRIUMPHANT POEM THAT CELEBRATES THE DESTRUCTION OF THE CITY OF NINEVEH, CAPITAL OF ASSYRIA. THE CITY FELL IN 612 BC AND FINISHED OFF THE ASSYRIANS.

> But surely it wasn't right for him to _rejoice_ about it?

NAHUM REJOICED FOR SEVERAL REASONS —

- THE END OF ASSYRIA MEANT LIBERATION FOR JUDAH
- THE ASSYRIANS WERE RECEIVING GOD'S JUDGMENT ON THEIR OWN CRUEL WAYS
- ASSYRIA'S DOWNFALL SHOWED THAT GOD HAD ULTIMATE CONTROL IN HISTORY

HABAKKUK

HABAKKUK IS A QUIETER BOOK THAN NAHUM. THE TRIUMPH OF NAHUM HAS NOW TURNED INTO SOMETHING CLOSE TO DESPAIR. ALTHOUGH THE ASSYRIANS ARE GONE, THEY'VE BEEN REPLACED BY THE BABYLONIANS (WHO WERE EVEN WORSE). HABAKKUK ASKS HOW GOD, WHO HATES EVIL, CAN ALLOW THE VIOLENT BABYLONIANS TO ATTACK AND DESTROY PEOPLE BETTER THAN THEMSELVES.

THE ANSWER HE GETS IN CHAPTER 2 IS THAT GOD'S JUDGMENT IS ON ITS WAY— SLOWLY, BUT INEVITABLY. HABAKKUK'S FAITH IN GOD IS RESTORED.

> Those who are evil will not survive, but those who are righteous will live because they are faithful to God.
>
> HABAKKUK 2:4

ZEPHANIAH

DO YOU KNOW ANYTHING ABOUT ZEPHANIAH?

YES. I BELIEVE HE HAD ROYAL BLOOD.

ZEPHANIAH WAS DESCENDED FROM KING HEZEKIAH OF JUDAH. HE PROPHESIED DURING THE REIGN OF KING JOSIAH (2 CHRONICLES 34-35) IN THE LAST FIFTY YEARS BEFORE JUDAH WAS DRAGGED OFF INTO EXILE. SINCE THE DAYS OF HEZEKIAH, JUDAH HAD SUNK DEEPER AND DEEPER INTO VIOLENCE AND THE WORSHIP OF IDOLS. THIS WAS TO BRING DOWN GOD'S ANGER (ZEPHANIAH 1).

The Day of the Lord

POPULAR BELIEF AT THAT TIME IN 'THE DAY OF THE LORD'. THIS WAS THE HOPE THAT ONE DAY SOON GOD WOULD STEP IN TO HELP THEM. THEIR ENEMIES WOULD BE CRUSHED, JUDAH WOULD RULE THE WORLD, EVERYONE WOULD BE FABULOUSLY RICH, THE HARVESTS WOULD BE MASSIVE, AND SO ON. IT DIDN'T MATTER (THEY THOUGHT) THAT JUDAH CONSTANTLY DISOBEYED GOD — HE WOULD JUST COME ALONG AND FIX IT FOR THEM. ZEPHANIAH SAVAGELY TURNED THIS THINKING ON ITS HEAD. ON THE DAY OF THE LORD, HE SAID, GOD WOULD JUDGE JUDAH TOO FOR ALL ITS SINS. AMOS HAD FIRST SAID THIS IN AMOS 5:18-20. ZEPHANIAH NOW DROVE THE MESSAGE HOME WITH A VENGEANCE.

ZEPHANIAH'S PROPHECIES MUST HAVE SHOCKED A LOT OF PEOPLE. THERE WAS A

> The great day of the Lord is near — it will be a day of fury, a day of trouble and distress, a day of ruin and destruction, a day of darkness and gloom, a black and cloudy day, a day filled with the sound of war-trumpets and the battle-cry of soldiers attacking fortified cities and high towers.
>
> ZEPHANIAH 1:14-16

Haggai Zechariah Malachi

THESE THREE BOOKS, ON THE VERY EDGE OF THE OLD TESTAMENT, HAD POWERFUL THINGS TO SAY TO THE PEOPLE OF THEIR TIME. IN THEM, THE PROPHETS ALSO STRAINED FORWARD TO SEE INTO THE NEW TESTAMENT. THEIR MESSAGES WERE GIVEN TO THE PEOPLE OF JUDAH AFTER THEY HAD RETURNED FROM EXILE. SO WHAT WERE THEY ABOUT?

HAGGAI THIS SMALL BOOK IS A COLLECTION OF PROPHECIES GIVEN IN 520 BC IN JERUSALEM. ITS MESSAGE IS SUMMED UP IN HAGGAI 1:4 — 'MY PEOPLE, WHY SHOULD YOU BE LIVING IN WELL-BUILT HOUSES WHILE MY TEMPLE LIES IN RUINS?' HAGGAI TOLD THEM TO GET ON WITH IT!

ZECHARIAH THESE PROPHECIES WERE GIVEN BETWEEN 520 AND 518 BC. IN CHAPTERS 1-8, ZECHARIAH RECEIVES VISIONS ABOUT JERUSALEM, THE NEW TEMPLE AND THE EXILES' RETURN. CHAPTERS 9-14 LOOK FORWARD TO THE FUTURE MESSIAH (SEE PAGE 101).

MALACHI BY HIS TIME, THE TEMPLE HAD BEEN FINISHED AND LIFE WAS SETTLED. BUT WORSHIP WAS ONCE AGAIN EMPTY, AND THE PEOPLE WERE DISOBEYING GOD. MALACHI WARNED OF GOD'S JUDGMENT, WHICH WOULD COME SUDDENLY.

PROPHECIES THAT POINT FORWARD TO THE NEW TESTAMENT:

I will send my messenger to prepare the way for me.

MALACHI 3:1
(SEE MATTHEW 11:10)

They will look on me, the one they have pierced, and mourn for him as one mourns for an only child...

ZECHARIAH 12:10
(SEE JOHN 19:37)

Shout for joy, you people of Jerusalem! Look, your king is coming to you! He comes triumphant and victorious, but humble and riding on a donkey — on a colt, the foal of a donkey.

ZECHARIAH 9:9
(SEE MATTHEW 21:1-11)

EXTRA BOOKS

WHAT BOOKS?

WHAT ARE THEY?

NOT EVERYONE AGREES WHICH BOOKS SHOULD BE INCLUDED, BUT HERE ARE THE ONES THAT ARE ALWAYS IN THE LIST...

- ☐ 1 + 2 MACCABEES
- ☐ TOBIT
- ☐ JUDITH
- ☐ EXTRA BITS ADDED TO THE OLD TESTAMENT BOOK OF ESTHER
- ☐ BOOK OF WISDOM
- ☐ ECCLESIASTICUS (BEN SIRA)
- ☐ BARUCH
- ☐ EXTRA BITS ADDED TO THE OLD TESTAMENT BOOK OF DANIEL

DISPUTED BOOKS INCLUDE 1 + 2 ESDRAS, LETTER OF JEREMIAH, PRAYER OF MANASSEH.

THESE ARE THE BOOKS MOST COMMONLY CALLED 'THE APOCRYPHA'. WRITTEN BETWEEN ABOUT 300 BC AND AD 100, THEY SPAN THE GAP BETWEEN THE OLD AND NEW TESTAMENTS. CHRISTIANS DISAGREE OVER THE EXACT STATUS OF THESE BOOKS. ARE THEY PART OF INSPIRED SCRIPTURE OR NOT?

 ROMAN CATHOLICS SAY 'YES' TO THIS, ALTHOUGH THEY CALL THE BOOKS 'DEUTERO-CANONICAL' WHICH MEANS THAT THEY ARE DRAWN FROM A SECOND LIST OF 'CANONICAL' (AUTHORITATIVE) BOOKS. IN CATHOLIC BIBLES, THESE BOOKS ARE SCATTERED IN APPROPRIATE PLACES THROUGHOUT THE OLD TESTAMENT.

 PROTESTANTS SAY 'NO'. THEY BELIEVE THAT THE BOOKS ARE NOT PART OF SCRIPTURE, BUT THAT THEY ARE USEFUL FOR READING BY CHRISTIANS. IN PROTESTANT BIBLES, THE APOCRYPHA IS EITHER LEFT OUT COMPLETELY, OR APPEARS IN A BLOCK BETWEEN THE OLD AND NEW TESTAMENTS.

CHRISTIANS ARE AGREED THAT THE BOOKS OF THE APOCRYPHA, CAREFULLY READ, ARE VALUABLE IN LINKING THE HISTORY OF THE OLD AND NEW TESTAMENTS, AND ALSO FOR THEIR WISDOM AND SPIRITUAL INSIGHT.

THE GOOD NEWS

THIS SECTION CONTAINS THE BOOKS OF...

MATTHEW, MARK, LUKE, JOHN, AND ACTS

THE GOOD NEWS

THIS SECTION OF THE BIBLE CONTAINS THE GOOD NEWS ABOUT JESUS CHRIST. THE FIRST FOUR BOOKS ARE THE GOSPELS OF MATTHEW, MARK, LUKE AND JOHN ('GOSPEL' IS AN OLD ENGLISH WORD MEANING 'GOOD NEWS'). THESE GIVE FOUR DIFFERENT ACCOUNTS OF THE LIFE, TEACHING AND DEATH OF JESUS. THE FIFTH BOOK IS KNOWN AS 'ACTS', BUT ITS FULL TITLE IS 'THE ACTS OF THE APOSTLES'. THIS TELLS THE STORY OF THE FIRST CHRISTIANS AND GIVES THE EXPLOITS OF THE 'APOSTLES' (THE PEOPLE SENT OUT SPECIFICALLY BY JESUS TO SPREAD HIS GOOD NEWS).

Sorry to stop you - but can we go back a bit? What exactly is this good news?

WELL, TO TAKE JUST THREE SMALL CHUNKS FROM THESE BOOKS...

> They will call him Immanuel - which means 'God with us'.
>
> MATTHEW 1:23

JESUS WASN'T JUST A MESSENGER FROM GOD. HE WAS GOD HIMSELF, LIVING A FULLY HUMAN LIFE.

> The Son of Man did not come to be served, but to serve, and to give his life as a ransom for many.
>
> MARK 10:45

THE WHOLE POINT OF JESUS' LIFE WAS THAT HE CAME TO SERVE PEOPLE. HE HEALED THE SICK, GAVE THE BLIND SIGHT — AND HE MADE IT POSSIBLE FOR PEOPLE TO BE FORGIVEN AND COME HOME TO GOD.

> God raised Jesus from death, setting him free from its power, because it was impossible that death should hold him prisoner.
>
> ACTS 2:24

THE MOST IMPORTANT THING JESUS DID WAS TO DIE ON THE CROSS. HE ENTERED INTO THE HUMAN EXPERIENCE OF DEATH (WHICH CAME ABOUT BECAUSE OF EVIL IN THE WORLD). BY HIS RESURRECTION, HE DESTROYED THE POWER OF DEATH FOR EVERYONE WHO BELIEVES IN HIM.

NOW, WHERE WERE WE?

What I can't understand is why we have <u>four</u> Gospels! Surely <u>one</u> would do?

Try thinking of it like this: Suppose you were interested in moving to a different town, and you wanted to know what it was like there. Which would be better—talking to just one person who lived there, or to four? In the same way, the four accounts of Jesus' life give us a fuller picture of what he was like.

EACH GOSPEL GIVES US A DIFFERENT ANGLE ON WHO JESUS WAS...

MATTHEW

WRITTEN FOR PEOPLE WITH A JEWISH BACKGROUND. THIS GOSPEL SHOWS HOW JESUS FULFILLED ALL THE LONGINGS OF THE OLD TESTAMENT. IT ALSO HAS PLENTY OF JESUS' PRACTICAL TEACHING FOR LIFE.

MARK

WRITTEN TO INTRODUCE PEOPLE TO JESUS FOR THE FIRST TIME. MARK MAY WELL BE THE EARLIEST OF THE FOUR GOSPELS. IT'S FULL OF ACTION, AND CHALLENGES THE READER TO DECIDE ABOUT JESUS.

LUKE

WRITTEN TO GIVE PEOPLE A FULL, COMPREHENSIVE RECORD OF JESUS. LUKE DID A LOT OF RESEARCH TO GET HIS FACTS STRAIGHT. HE PARTICULARLY SHOWS JESUS' LOVE FOR ORDINARY, DISADVANTAGED PEOPLE.

JOHN

WRITTEN FOR THOSE WHO ALREADY KNOW THE FACTS ABOUT JESUS, BUT WHO ARE PUZZLED AS TO WHAT IT ALL MEANS. JOHN DRAWS OUT THE DEEP SIGNIFICANCE OF JESUS' LIFE.

PHUT!

MATTHEW, MARK, LUKE AND JOHN AREN'T JUST BIOGRAPHIES OF JESUS – THEY'RE DIFFERENT:

■ THEY SPEND ALMOST HALF THE TIME ON THE EVENTS LEADING TO JESUS' DEATH. THEY SAW HIS DEATH AS THE KEY TO UNDERSTANDING HIM.

■ THEY ARE TALKING ABOUT SOMEONE WHO IS STILL ALIVE. THEY AIM TO GET THEIR READERS TO MEET JESUS FOR THEMSELVES.

MATTHEW

MATTHEW'S GOSPEL IS THE FIRST BOOK IN THE NEW TESTAMENT, AND SO IT'S NEAREST (IN TERMS OF PAGES) TO THE OLD TESTAMENT. THIS IS APPROPRIATE, BECAUSE MATTHEW, MORE THAN MARK, LUKE OR JOHN, SHOWS THAT JESUS IS THE FULFILMENT OF THE OLD TESTAMENT HOPE FOR A MESSIAH (SEE PAGE 101). MATTHEW WROTE TO SHOW HIS JEWISH READERS THAT FAITH IN JESUS WAS QUITE NATURAL FOR ANY JEW, AS JESUS' LIFE AND TEACHING CAME FROM DEEP JEWISH ROOTS.

That's remarkable! But how does he do it?

1 WELL FIRST, MATTHEW KEEPS QUOTING PASSAGES FROM THE OLD TESTAMENT PROPHETS AND PSALMS, AND THEN SAYING HOW THE LIFE AND TEACHING OF JESUS FITS THEM LIKE A GLOVE. HERE'S A TYPICAL EXAMPLE WHICH COMES AFTER JESUS HAD BEEN HEALING SICK PEOPLE...

66 This was to fulfill what was spoken through the prophet Isaiah: 'He took up our infirmities and carried our diseases.' 99 MATTHEW 8:17

HERE ARE SOME OF THE OTHER INSTANCES OF THIS. THE POINT MATTHEW WAS MAKING WAS THAT THE GOD OF ISRAEL WAS IN CONTROL OF JESUS' LIFE. IT WAS ALL HAPPENING AS HAD LONG AGO BEEN PREDICTED.

MATTHEW 1:23
JESUS IS IMMANUEL – 'GOD WITH US'

MATTHEW 2:18
THE KILLING OF BETHLEHEM'S CHILDREN

MATTHEW 2:23
JESUS IS TO BE BROUGHT UP IN NAZARETH

MATTHEW 4:15-16
JESUS PREACHES IN GALILEE

MATTHEW 12:18-20
JESUS AS GOD'S SERVANT

MATTHEW 13:35
WHY JESUS USED PARABLES

MATTHEW 21:5
JESUS ENTERS JERUSALEM RIDING ON A DONKEY

MATTHEW 27:9-10
HOW JUDAS'S BLOOD MONEY WAS SPENT

2 THE JEWISH PEOPLE EXPECTED THE MESSIAH TO FULFILL OR DEEPEN THE LAW OF MOSES. MATTHEW SHOWS JESUS THE JEWISH MESSIAH DOING EXACTLY THAT. FOR EXAMPLE...

> Do not think that I have come to abolish the Law or the Prophets; I have not come to abolish them but to fulfill them.

MATTHEW 5:17

MATTHEW PAINTS A STRIKING PICTURE OF JESUS AS THE GREAT TEACHER, TELLING THE PEOPLE, WITH AUTHORITY, WHAT THE REAL MEANING OF THE OLD TESTAMENT LAW IS. THIS IS ESPECIALLY HIGHLIGHTED IN THE SERMON ON THE MOUNT (SEE MATTHEW 5:21-48).

3 AND JUST TO MAKE HIS POINT CRYSTAL CLEAR, MATTHEW PUTS JESUS' TEACHING INTO FIVE SEPARATE BLOCKS OF TEXT. HE DOES THIS TO DRAW A PARALLEL WITH THE FIVE BOOKS OF THE LAW OF MOSES (GENESIS TO DEUTERONOMY). THE FIRST BLOCK OF TEACHING IS EVEN GIVEN ON A MOUNTAIN, JUST AS MOSES WAS ON MOUNT SINAI. IN THIS WAY, HE SHOWED THAT JESUS FULFILLED THE LAW AND THE PROPHETS – THE HEART OF THE OLD TESTAMENT.

THOSE FIVE BLOCKS

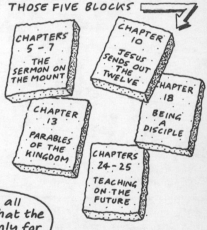

CHAPTERS 5 - 7 THE SERMON ON THE MOUNT

CHAPTER 10 JESUS SENDS OUT THE TWELVE

CHAPTER 18 BEING A DISCIPLE

CHAPTER 13 PARABLES OF THE KINGDOM

CHAPTERS 24 - 25 TEACHING ON THE FUTURE

> But does all that mean that the good news is only for Jewish people?

NO. THE GOOD NEWS GROWS OUT OF WHAT GOD DID IN THE OLD TESTAMENT, BUT IT'S GOOD NEWS FOR THE WHOLE WORLD – FOR JEWS AND NON-JEWS (GENTILES). MATTHEW MAKES THIS CLEAR IN MATTHEW 8:5-13 AND 21:33-46. AND HIS BOOK CLOSES WITH THESE WORDS:

> Go and make disciples of all nations...

MATTHEW 28:19

93

DID IT REALLY HAPPEN?

SOME PEOPLE HAVE SAID THAT JESUS NEVER EXISTED. OR THAT IF HE DID, HIS LIFE WAS VERY DIFFERENT FROM WHAT THE NEW TESTAMENT TELLS US. THEY SAY THAT HIS FOLLOWERS EXAGGERATED ABOUT HIM, ADDING DETAILS THAT NEVER TOOK PLACE...

THIS WAY

YES, I MEAN— HEALING THE SICK, CALMING A STORM, WALKING ON WATER, SAYING HE WAS GOD'S SON — THEY ALL MAKE A GREAT STORY, BUT DID IT REALLY HAPPEN? WHAT'S THE EVIDENCE?

OUR MAIN SOURCES OF INFORMATION FOR THE LIFE OF JESUS COME FROM THE NEW TESTAMENT ITSELF. FROM WHAT WE KNOW OF THE AUTHORS, EVERYTHING SUGGESTS THAT THEY WERE TRUTHFUL, RELIABLE PEOPLE, WHO WERE EVEN WILLING TO DIE FOR WHAT THEY SAID HAD HAPPENED. ONE WRITER, LUKE, WAS A WELL-RESEARCHED HISTORIAN.

BUT IT ALL TOOK PLACE 2,000 <u>YEARS</u> AGO! HOW DO WE KNOW THAT IT'S COME DOWN TO US ACCURATELY?

THE COPIES WE HAVE OF THE NEW TESTAMENT BOOKS ARE VERY OLD. THEY'RE LIKELY TO BE ACCURATE COPIES AS THEY ARE SO CLOSE TO THE TIME THEY WERE FIRST WRITTEN. LOOK AT THIS... HISTORIANS ACCEPT THAT THE COPY WE HAVE OF 'THE GALLIC WAR' BY CAESAR IS ACCURATE. YET THERE'S A 900 YEAR GAP!

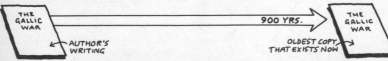

THE GALLIC WAR — AUTHOR'S WRITING — 900 YRS. — THE GALLIC WAR — OLDEST COPY THAT EXISTS NOW

NOW HERE'S THE NEW TESTAMENT. THERE ARE 3,000 GREEK MANUSCRIPTS FOR IT — FOR CAESAR'S BOOK THERE ARE ONLY TEN!

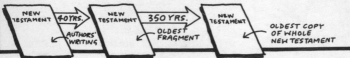

NEW TESTAMENT — 40 YRS. AUTHORS' WRITING — NEW TESTAMENT — 350 YRS. OLDEST FRAGMENT — NEW TESTAMENT — OLDEST COPY OF WHOLE NEW TESTAMENT

YES, THERE WERE. ONE SUCH WRITER WAS JOSEPHUS, THE JEWISH HISTORIAN. HE WROTE:

"AND THERE AROSE ABOUT THIS TIME JESUS, A WISE MAN, IF INDEED WE SHOULD CALL HIM A MAN; FOR HE WAS A DOER OF MARVELLOUS DEEDS, A TEACHER OF MEN WHO RECEIVE THE TRUTH WITH PLEASURE. HE LED AWAY MANY JEWS, AND ALSO MANY OF THE GREEKS. THIS MAN WAS THE CHRIST. AND WHEN PILATE HAD CONDEMNED HIM TO THE CROSS ON HIS IMPEACHMENT BY THE CHIEF MEN AMONG US, THOSE WHO HAD LOVED HIM AT FIRST DID NOT CEASE; FOR HE APPEARED TO THEM ON THE THIRD DAY ALIVE AGAIN... AND EVEN NOW THE TRIBE OF CHRISTIANS, SO NAMED AFTER HIM, HAS NOT YET DIED OUT." WRITTEN AD 93

BUT WERE THERE ANY NON-CHRISTIAN WRITERS TO SAY THAT JESUS EXISTED?

Tacitus

HE WAS A ROMAN WRITER (AND CERTAINLY NO FRIEND TO CHRISTIANS!) HE CONFIRMED THAT JESUS HAD STARTED SOMETHING BIG...

JOT THIS DOWN, MISS VELLUM:

"THE NAME CHRISTIAN COMES FROM CHRIST, WHO WAS EXECUTED IN THE REIGN OF TIBERIUS BY THE PROCURATOR PONTIUS PILATE; AND THE PERNICIOUS SUPERSTITION, SUPPRESSED FOR A WHILE, BROKE OUT AFRESH AND SPREAD NOT ONLY THROUGH JUDEA, THE SOURCE OF THE MALADY, BUT EVEN THROUGHOUT ROME ITSELF, WHERE EVERYTHING VILE COMES AND IS FETED." WRITTEN AD 114

GOSH!

ANOTHER WRITER SAID—

ON THE EVE OF THE PASSOVER, THEY HANGED JESHUA OF NAZARETH.

JUDGE THE EVIDENCE FOR YOURSELF...

12 DISCIPLES

I honestly don't know why Jesus bothered with the disciples! They didn't understand him half the time!

Yes, the disciples were almost as imperfect as we are! But he chose them for a special reason...

66 THAT THEY MIGHT BE WITH HIM AND THAT HE MIGHT SEND THEM OUT TO PREACH AND TO HAVE AUTHORITY TO DRIVE OUT DEMONS. 99
MARK 3:14-15

In other words, Jesus was training them to do his work.

HERE'S A QUICK INTRODUCTION TO ALL TWELVE DISCIPLES:

SIMON PETER WITH JAMES AND JOHN, PETER WAS ONE OF THE THREE WHO WERE CLOSEST TO JESUS. HIS FAITH WAS STRONG, BUT HE WAS RASH AND HOT-HEADED AT TIMES. SEE PAGE 116.

JAMES BROTHER OF JOHN. THEY WERE BOTH FISHERMEN.

JOHN JOHN WAS CLOSEST OF ALL TO JESUS. AFTER JESUS' RESURRECTION, HE AND PETER LED THE JERUSALEM CHURCH. FOR MORE ON JAMES AND JOHN, SEE PAGE 100.

ANDREW PETER'S BROTHER. THEY TOO WERE FISHERMEN.

PHILIP CAME FROM GALILEE. HE ASKED LOTS OF QUESTIONS ABOUT WHO JESUS WAS.

BARTHOLOMEW PROBABLY ALSO KNOWN AS NATHANAEL.

MATTHEW A TAXMAN WHO LEFT HIS WELL-PAID JOB TO FOLLOW JESUS. ALSO KNOWN AS LEVI.

THOMAS BETTER KNOWN AS 'DOUBTING THOMAS' FOR WHAT HE DID IN JOHN 20:24-29.

JAMES (SON OF ALPHAEUS). NOTHING'S KNOWN ABOUT HIM.

SIMON (THE ZEALOT). PROBABLY ATTACHED TO A GROUP OF TERRORISTS BEFORE MEETING JESUS.

JUDAS (SON OF JAMES). ALSO KNOWN AS THADDAEUS.

JUDAS (ISCARIOT). THE ONE WHO BETRAYED JESUS TO HIS ENEMIES. AFTER JESUS' DEATH, HE COMMITTED SUICIDE. SEE PAGE 113.

John the Baptist

> Where does John the Baptist fit into the story of Jesus?

THE BOOK OF MALACHI (SEE PAGE 87), WRITTEN OVER 400 YEARS BEFORE JESUS, SAID THAT BEFORE THE MESSIAH CAME, A PROPHET LIKE ELIJAH WOULD APPEAR TO PREPARE THE WAY FOR HIM:

66 ... I will send you the prophet Elijah. 99 MALACHI 4:5

JESUS SAID THAT JOHN THE BAPTIST WAS THIS PROPHET (MATTHEW 11:14). HE ALSO SAID THAT JOHN WAS THE GREATEST OF ALL ISRAEL'S PROPHETS (LUKE 7:18-35).

JOHN'S MESSAGE TO ISRAEL WAS QUITE SIMPLE...

REPENT!

THIS IS A WORD THAT MEANS: 'GIVE UP SINNING AND COME BACK TO GOD!'

JOHN WAS JUST LIKE SOME OF THE OLD TESTAMENT PROPHETS. HIS MESSAGE WAS FIERY AND HARD-HITTING. HE LIVED OUT IN THE DESERT WEARING A ROUGH, CAMEL-HAIR CLOAK AND LEATHER BELT. HE LIVED ON A DIET OF LOCUSTS AND HONEY MADE BY VICIOUS DESERT BEES. HE MUST HAVE BEEN FORMIDABLE!

DIARY OF A LOCUST

eat, eat,
eat, eat,
splat!

CONCLUDED

JOHN BAPTIZED PEOPLE IN THE RIVER JORDAN AS A SIGN THAT THEY HAD BEEN FORGIVEN. BUT WHEN THE PHARISEES AND SADDUCEES CAME TO SEE HIM, HE GAVE THEM THE SHARP EDGE OF HIS TONGUE...

> You snakes! Who told you that you could escape from the punishment God is about to send?

MATTHEW 3:7

BUT WHEN JOHN ATTACKED THE CORRUPTION OF HEROD ANTIPAS, HE WAS THROWN INTO PRISON AND KILLED (MATTHEW 14:1-12). JOHN WAS IMPORTANT IN POINTING PEOPLE TO JESUS AS THE MESSIAH GOD HAD SENT. AFTER JOHN WAS IMPRISONED, JESUS BEGAN HIS WORK.

MARK

IS THIS POSE OKAY?

MARK'S GOSPEL IS THE SHORTEST OF THE FOUR ACCOUNTS OF JESUS' LIFE. IT'S A BOOK THAT IS FULL OF ACTION, AND MARK KEEPS THE EVENTS COMING SO THICK AND FAST THAT THEY ALMOST TREAD ON EACH OTHERS' TOES. IF THE FOUR GOSPELS WERE SOLD AS SEPARATE BOOKS IN A MODERN BOOKSHOP, LUKE MIGHT END UP ON THE POPULAR HISTORY SHELF, MATTHEW AND JOHN AMONG RELIGIOUS BOOKS, WHILE MARK WOULD BE IN AMONGST THE THRILLERS! SO IF YOU'VE NEVER READ A GOSPEL, TRY THIS ONE...

Mark gets straight to the point about Jesus Christ. Unlike Matthew and Luke, he doesn't give us any long birth stories, but plunges in with John the Baptist. The story moves so quickly that by verse 16 of chapter 1, Jesus is already picking his disciples! It's a blunt, unforgettable picture of Jesus.

THIS WAY

SO WHO WROTE IT?

THERE IS STRONG EVIDENCE TO SUGGEST THAT IT WAS JOHN MARK, A FOLLOWER OF JESUS. THE EARLY CHRISTIANS USED TO MEET IN THE HOUSE OF MARK'S MOTHER IN JERUSALEM. MARK LATER JOURNEYED WITH PAUL, BUT ABANDONED HIM, WHICH CAUSED A RIFT BETWEEN THEM FOR A WHILE (ACTS 13:13). LATER, MARK WAS REUNITED WITH PAUL AND WAS WITH HIM IN ROME (COLOSSIANS 4:10). TWO MORE THINGS ABOUT MARK:

- IT'S RECKONED HE WROTE HIMSELF INTO HIS GOSPEL AS THE STREAKER IN MARK 14:51-52...
- MARK HAD A NICKNAME. IT WAS <u>KOLOBODAKTYLOS</u>, MEANING, 'STUMPY-FINGERS'!

MARK'S MOST IMPORTANT RELATIONSHIP, THOUGH, WAS WITH THE APOSTLE PETER. 1 PETER 5:13 TELLS US THEY WERE TOGETHER IN ROME, WHERE MARK WAS PETER'S HELPER.

MARK PROBABLY RELIED ON PETER'S MEMORIES OF JESUS TO WRITE HIS BOOK. A CHURCH LEADER CALLED PAPIAS WROTE THESE WORDS IN AD 140...

 THIS WAY

66 Mark, being the interpreter of Peter, Wrote accurately (though not in order) all that he remembered of what was either said or done by the Lord... 99

If Mark _did_ write from Peter's memories, then the stories would sound like eyewitness accounts...

Which they do! Just look at Mark 7:32-35 and Mark 8:22-26!

And also, if they were _Peter's_ stories, you'd expect them to be as he would tell them — full of action, hurrying from one story to the next. Which is exactly how Mark's Gospel is.

MARK'S GOSPEL SPOTLIGHTS TWO VERY IMPORTANT CHARACTERISTICS OF WHO JESUS WAS:

1 Human Being

MARK SHOWS US THE HUMAN JESUS. JESUS SO HEAVILY ASLEEP THROUGH EXHAUSTION THAT EVEN A STORM DOESN'T WAKE HIM (MARK 4:35-41). JESUS GETTING EXASPERATED AT HIS DISCIPLES FOR BEING SO SLOW TO UNDERSTAND (MARK 8:14-21). JESUS JUST BEFORE HIS ARREST, RETURNING TO HIS DISCIPLES AGAIN AND AGAIN FOR HUMAN COMPANY, ONLY TO FIND THEM ASLEEP (MARK 14:32-42).

2 Son of God

MARK ALSO SHOWS US JESUS AS THE SON OF GOD. MARK IS AN EASTERN BOOK, IN WHICH THE BEGINNING, MIDDLE AND END ARE _THE_ KEY PLACES TO GIVE THE MEANING OF THE WHOLE BOOK. IN THESE THREE KEY PLACES IN MARK, JESUS IS DECLARED TO BE THE SON OF GOD. THIS HAPPENS AT HIS BAPTISM (MARK 1:11); AT HIS TRANSFIGURATION (MARK 9:7); AND AT THE SCENE OF HIS CRUCIFIXION (MARK 15:39).

MARK CLEARLY ARRANGED HIS MATERIAL TO SAY TO THE READER: 'LOOK! THIS JESUS WAS GOD'S SON. FOLLOW HIM!'

James + John

WHEN JESUS CALLED JAMES AND JOHN TO BE HIS DISCIPLES, THEY WERE TWO ORDINARY FISHERMEN. HE NICKNAMED THEM 'THE SONS OF THUNDER'.

High voltage characters, eh?

TWO INCIDENTS TELL US ABOUT THE FIERY CHARACTER OF JAMES AND JOHN. IN MARK 10:35-45 THEY ASKED JESUS FOR THE BEST PLACES IN HIS KINGDOM. AND IN LUKE 9:51-56 THEY WANTED TO CALL DOWN FIRE FROM HEAVEN ON A VILLAGE THAT WOULDN'T WELCOME JESUS.

THE THREE

DESPITE THEIR HOT TEMPERAMENTS (OR PERHAPS BECAUSE OF THEM!), JAMES AND JOHN, TOGETHER WITH PETER, WERE THE CLOSEST TO JESUS. ON THREE IMPORTANT OCCASIONS, THESE THREE DISCIPLES WERE MENTIONED:

- MARK 5:35-43 JESUS RAISES JAIRUS'S DAUGHTER
- MARK 9:2-9 JESUS IS TRANSFIGURED
- MARK 14:32-42 JESUS PRAYS BEFORE HIS DEATH

John

JOHN, OF ALL THE DISCIPLES, WAS CLOSEST TO JESUS. HE IS IDENTIFIED AS THE CRYPTICALLY-NAMED 'DISCIPLE WHOM JESUS LOVED' IN JOHN'S GOSPEL.

AFTER JESUS WAS RAISED FROM DEATH, JOHN AND PETER LED THE JERUSALEM CHURCH (SEE ACTS 3-4).

ACCORDING TO SECOND-CENTURY WRITERS, JOHN DIED A VERY OLD MAN IN EPHESUS. SOME PEOPLE THINK JOHN WAS THE WRITER OF THE BOOK OF REVELATION. IF SO, THEN JOHN ALSO SPENT TIME EXILED ON THE ISLAND OF PATMOS.

James

OUT OF PETER, JAMES AND JOHN, JAMES WAS THIRD IN CLOSENESS TO JESUS. IN ACTS 12:2, JAMES WAS 'PUT TO DEATH BY THE SWORD' BY KING HEROD AGRIPPA I. THIS HAPPENED ABOUT AD 44, FOURTEEN YEARS AFTER JESUS' DEATH.

MESSIAH

'MESSIAH' IS A HEBREW WORD. THE GREEK VERSION OF IT IS 'CHRIST'. BOTH OF THESE WORDS MEAN 'A PERSON WHO HAS BEEN ANOINTED BY GOD'.

IN THE OLD TESTAMENT, KINGS WERE ANOINTED WITH OIL (IT WAS POURED ON THEIR HEADS) AT THEIR CORONATION. SAMUEL CROWNED SAUL IN THIS WAY (1 SAMUEL 10:1). THIS WAS DONE TO SYMBOLIZE THAT GOD GAVE THE KING HIS POWER TO RULE WISELY AND JUSTLY, AND TO CARRY OUT GOD'S PURPOSES.

KING DAVID

David was Israel's greatest king. But he was followed by a line of weak or evil rulers which was ended by the exile in Babylon (see page 74). So the Jewish people began to hope for a great ruler, the Messiah, descended from King David. God would send him at the end of history to save them from their enemies and to rule them with justice.

HOW THE OLD TESTAMENT SAW THE MESSIAH...

ISAIAH 9:2-7
THE PRINCE OF PEACE

ISAIAH 11:1-9
THE MESSIAH'S RULE

EZEKIEL 37:24-25
A KING LIKE DAVID TO RULE FOR EVER

PSALM 2
THE SCOURGE OF THE NATIONS

THAT'S WHAT HE'LL DO TO THE GREEKS!

UP TO THE TIME OF JESUS, ISRAEL WAS RULED HARSHLY BY THE GREEKS AND THEN BY THE ROMANS. THE JEWS NOW SAW THE COMING MESSIAH AS A WARRIOR-KING WHO WOULD DESTROY ISRAEL'S OPPRESSORS. THIS IS WHY JESUS WAS VERY CAUTIOUS IN HIS OWN LIFETIME ABOUT BEING CALLED THE MESSIAH. BUT HIS FOLLOWERS PROCLAIMED THAT HE WAS DESCENDED FROM DAVID (SEE MATTHEW 1:1) AND THAT HE WAS ISRAEL'S TRUE MESSIAH. THIS IS WHY HE IS STILL KNOWN AS JESUS CHRIST.

Miracles

IF YOU OPEN MATTHEW, MARK OR LUKE AT ALMOST ANY PAGE, YOU CAN'T HELP FINDING THE STORY OF A MIRACLE JESUS DID. HE BROUGHT SIGHT TO BLIND PEOPLE, TURNED WATER INTO WINE, CALMED A STORM AND HEALED ILLNESSES.

> But do we _have_ to believe in Jesus' miracles? Why not just forget about them and have a non-miraculous Jesus?

BECAUSE IT'S IMPOSSIBLE TO CUT OUT OF THE GOSPELS THE MIRACLES OF JESUS WITHOUT LEAVING THEM IN SHREDS! ALMOST ONE-THIRD OF MARK'S GOSPEL DEALS WITH MIRACLES BROUGHT ABOUT BY JESUS. THE MIRACLES WERE CENTRAL TO HIS LIFE.

> But hasn't science disproved miracles? They'd break the laws of nature!

> Which could be _very_ unpleasant!

THE 'LAWS' OF NATURE ARE ONLY WAYS TO DESCRIBE WHAT NORMALLY HAPPENS. TO SAY, 'THE LAWS OF NATURE CAN _NEVER_ BE BROKEN' ISN'T A SCIENTIFIC STATEMENT BUT A STATEMENT OF FAITH. IN ABNORMAL CONDITIONS (SUCH AS IN A MIRACLE) THESE 'LAWS' MAY BE TEMPORARILY SUSPENDED BY THE GOD WHO MADE THEM IN THE FIRST PLACE.

> But in those days, great people were expected to do miracles. Isn't this why the first Christians invented these stories about Jesus?

YES, THERE WERE MANY 'MIRACLE-WORKERS' AROUND THEN. BUT JESUS' MIRACLES WERE VERY DIFFERENT. HE DIDN'T USE MAGICAL WORDS OR ACTIONS. HIS MIRACLES WERE MOTIVATED BY HIS LOVE FOR PEOPLE OR TO POINT PEOPLE TO GOD. AND JESUS WAS NO GREAT SHOWMAN OR ENTERTAINER, WANTING TO DRAW A CROWD TO SEE HIS IMPRESSIVE TRICKS. INSTEAD, HE OFTEN TOLD PEOPLE NOT EVEN TO TALK ABOUT WHAT THEY HAD SEEN HIM DO (SEE MARK 5:43).

So why did Jesus do miracles anyway?

Matthew, Mark, Luke

IN THE FIRST THREE GOSPELS, THE MIRACLES ARE CALLED 'ACTS OF POWER'. JESUS DID THEM BECAUSE THEY PLAYED AN ESSENTIAL PART AS GOD'S KINGDOM BROKE INTO THE WORLD. JESUS HAD COME TO CONFRONT THE POWERS OF EVIL THAT HAD DAMAGED THE WORLD GOD HAD MADE. THIS DAMAGE COULD BE SEEN IN ILLNESSES, PEOPLE POSSESSED BY OCCULT POWERS, AND ULTIMATELY IN DEATH ITSELF. JESUS' MIRACLES WERE MIGHTY ACTS TO REVERSE ALL THIS AND TO REPAIR THE DAMAGE. THE MIRACLES WERE LIKE THE BLOWS OF A GREAT BATTERING-RAM AGAINST THE KINGDOM OF EVIL.

And John?

JOHN'S GOSPEL IS DIFFERENT. JOHN RECORDS ONLY SEVEN MIRACLES OF JESUS, AND UNLIKE MATTHEW, MARK AND LUKE, HE CALLS THEM 'SIGNS'. HERE JESUS' MIRACLES DON'T ONLY SHOW THAT GOD'S KINGDOM HAS ARRIVED IN POWER, BUT THAT THE KING HIMSELF HAS COME — IN THE PERSON OF JESUS. THE MIRACLES POINT TO JESUS AS SIGNS, TO HELP PEOPLE BELIEVE IN HIM AS GOD'S SON.

Give us an example!

HERE ARE A FEW: JESUS FED 5,000 PEOPLE MIRACULOUSLY, AND LATER SAID, 'I AM THE BREAD OF LIFE'. BEFORE HE HEALED A BLIND MAN HE SAID, 'I AM THE LIGHT OF THE WORLD'. AND BEFORE HE RAISED DEAD LAZARUS BACK TO LIFE, HE SAID, 'I AM THE RESURRECTION AND THE LIFE'. EACH OF THESE SIGNS REVEALS SOMETHING OF WHO JESUS WAS.

WHERE TO FIND THEM...

HEALING
PARALYSED MAN MARK 2:3-12
BARTIMAEUS MARK 10:46-52
CENTURION'S SERVANT LUKE 7:1-10
DEAF, DUMB MAN MARK 7:31-37
BLIND MAN MARK 8:22-26

CASTING OUT DEMONS
MAN FROM GADARA MARK 5:1-15
DUMB MAN MATTHEW 9:32-33

RAISING THE DEAD
LAZARUS JOHN 11:1-44
JAIRUS'S DAUGHTER MARK 5:22-24, 35-43

POWER OVER NATURE
CALMING A STORM MATTHEW 8:23-27
WALKING ON WATER JOHN 6:19-21
FEEDING 5,000 MARK 6:35-44

THE RESURRECTION
THE GREATEST OF ALL THE MIRACLES! MATTHEW 28, MARK 16, LUKE 24, JOHN 20

LUKE

LUKE'S GOSPEL IS THE FIRST BOOK IN A TWO-BOOK SET. THE BOOK OF ACTS IS THE COMPANION VOLUME (ALSO FROM THE PEN OF LUKE) AND IT CONTINUES THE STORY AFTER THE ASCENSION OF JESUS, LOOKING AT THE LIFE OF THE EARLY CHURCH.
SO ONCE YOU'VE FINISHED READING LUKE 24, CARRY ON WITH ACTS 1...

So, tell us about the author of these books

ALL THE EARLIEST CHURCH TRADITIONS AGREE THAT THE AUTHOR WAS LUKE, A DOCTOR WHO WAS A COMPANION OF PAUL ON HIS JOURNEYS. HIS AIM WAS TO WRITE AN ACCOUNT OF JESUS' LIFE THAT WAS HISTORICALLY ACCURATE, AND THAT COMMUNICATED WITH NON-JEWISH READERS (HE WAS A GENTILE HIMSELF).

AS LUKE COLLECTED THE STORIES ABOUT JESUS AND STARTED TO WRITE THEM INTO HIS GOSPEL, HE WAS ESPECIALLY CONCERNED TO SHOW HOW JESUS HAD LOVED AND CARED FOR THE POOR AND THE WEAK IN SOCIETY. IT WAS THEM, RATHER THAN THE RICH AND POWERFUL, WHO WERE CLOSEST TO RECEIVING THE GOOD NEWS. LUKE SPELLS THIS OUT IN TWO IMPORTANT PLACES AT THE BEGINNING OF HIS BOOK:

AND AT THE START OF HIS WORK, JESUS SAYS...

The Spirit of the Lord is upon me, because he has chosen me to bring good news to the poor.

LUKE 4:18

AT JESUS' CONCEPTION, MARY SINGS...

He has filled the hungry with good things, and sent the rich away with empty hands.

LUKE 1:53

So did that mean that the rich were left out?

NO- SOME OF THEM DID RESPOND TO JESUS. BUT THEY FIRST HAD TO HUMBLE THEMSELVES AND HAVE A REAL CHANGE OF HEART AND LIVING.

LUKE CONCENTRATES ON AT LEAST THREE GROUPS OF THE POWERLESS: THE POOR, SOCIAL OUTCASTS, AND WOMEN. THE EXAMPLES BELOW ARE TOLD <u>ONLY</u> BY LUKE — THEY DON'T APPEAR IN MATTHEW, MARK OR JOHN.

1 The Poor

IN LUKE, JESUS REVERSES THE ORDER OF SOCIAL PRIORITIES WHERE THE RICH ARE VIPs AND THE POOR DON'T MATTER.

THE PARABLES OF THE RICH FOOL (LUKE 12:16-21) AND LAZARUS (LUKE 16:19-31) REVEAL THE DEADLY DANGER OF WEALTH IN THE MOST CHILLING WAYS. ZACCHAEUS, A RICH AND CORRUPT TAXMAN (IN LUKE 19) FINDS SALVATION ONLY WHEN HE HAS GIVEN HALF HIS POSSESSIONS TO THE POOR, AND HAS PROMISED TO PAY BACK WITH INTEREST THE PEOPLE HE'S CHEATED.

> Instead, the rich are challenged to give up a way of life that makes it impossible for them to enter the Kingdom of God.

2 Outcasts

JESUS WAS INFAMOUS FOR MIXING WITH THE IMMORAL AND CRIMINAL ELEMENTS IN SOCIETY. HE DEFENDED HIMSELF BY SAYING THAT THESE WERE THE PEOPLE WHO MOST NEEDED HIS HELP. THREE OF LUKE'S EXAMPLES SHOW JESUS' ATTITUDE TO THE OUTCASTS OF HIS TIME...

- TAXMEN (WHO WERE HATED FOR THEIR GREED) LUKE 18:9-14
- SAMARITANS (A RACIAL GROUP RELATED TO THE JEWISH PEOPLE, BUT HATED BY THEM) LUKE 10:30-37
- LEPERS (WHO WERE FEARED AND DRIVEN OUT OF THE COMMUNITY) LUKE 17:11-19

3 Women

WOMEN IN JESUS' DAY WERE SEEN BY MEN AS GROSSLY INFERIOR. THEY WEREN'T ALLOWED TO TESTIFY IN COURT, AND NO ONE BOTHERED TO EDUCATE THEM.

> Do not talk to a woman in the street. No, not even with your own wife!

ADVICE BY A JEWISH RELIGIOUS TEACHER

BUT JESUS TREATED WOMEN DIFFERENTLY. HE TAUGHT THEM ALONGSIDE THE MEN (LUKE 10:38-42). LUKE MORE THAN ANYONE ELSE SHOWS US JESUS' COMPASSION FOR WOMEN (SEE LUKE 7:36-50).

IN THESE WAYS, LUKE SHOWS US GOD'S LOVE FOR THE DESPISED.

MARY

MARY (THE MOTHER OF JESUS) WAS ENGAGED TO JOSEPH WHEN SHE WAS VISITED BY ONE OF GOD'S SENIOR MESSENGERS, THE ANGEL GABRIEL. SHE WOULD HAVE BEEN SOMEWHERE BETWEEN THIRTEEN AND EIGHTEEN YEARS OLD (JEWISH MARRYING AGE). THE ANGEL BROUGHT HER DISTURBING NEWS:

But what about this Virgin Birth business?

> You will become pregnant and give birth to a son, and you will name him Jesus.
>
> LUKE 1:31

MARY'S FAITH WAS SO STRONG THAT SHE WAS ABLE HUMBLY TO ACCEPT THIS NEWS, DESPITE THE DISGRACE IT WOULD BRING TO HER AS AN UNMARRIED, PREGNANT GIRL. SEE LUKE 1:46-55 FOR HER RESPONSE.

KEY EVENTS

- MARY IS TOLD SHE WILL HAVE A SON LUKE 1:26-56
- THE BIRTH OF JESUS MATTHEW 1:18-25
- JOSEPH AND MARY PRESENT JESUS IN THE TEMPLE LUKE 2:22-40
- JESUS IN CHILDHOOD LUKE 2:41-52
- MARY AT CANA JOHN 2:1-12
- MARY AT THE CRUCIFIXION JOHN 19:25-27
- MARY IN THE EARLY CHURCH ACTS 1:14

1 IN LUKE 1:30-35 AND MATTHEW 1:18-25 JESUS IS SAID TO HAVE BEEN CONCEIVED WITHOUT A HUMAN FATHER, THROUGH THE WORK OF GOD'S SPIRIT. JESUS WAS THEREFORE (AS ONE EARLY WRITER PUT IT) 'THE SON OF MARY AND THE SON OF GOD'.

THE MEANING OF ALL THIS FOCUSES ON WHAT GOD WAS GOING TO DO THROUGH JESUS. JESUS CAME AS THE 'SECOND ADAM', THE HEAD OF A NEW HUMANITY, TO REDEEM ALL THE MISTAKES SET IN MOTION BY THE FIRST ADAM (SEE I CORINTHIANS 15:47-49). SO THIS RADICALLY DIFFERENT BIRTH WOULD BE APPROPRIATE BOTH TO WHO JESUS WAS AND TO WHAT HE CAME TO DO.

2 THE MIRACLE OF THE VIRGIN BIRTH IS ONLY A PART OF THE GREATER MIRACLE OF GOD BECOMING A HUMAN BEING, IN THE COMING OF JESUS. IF WE CAN ACCEPT THIS GREATER MIRACLE, THEN THE WAY IN WHICH IT TOOK PLACE IS JUST A DETAIL.

parables

JESUS GAVE A LOT OF HIS TEACHING IN PARABLES. THIS WORD 'PARABLE' HAS MANY MEANINGS: PICTURE, SYMBOL, RIDDLE, ALLEGORY, STORY WITH A HIDDEN MEANING... JESUS WASN'T THE FIRST TO USE PARABLES. JOTHAM USED ONE IN JUDGES 9, NATHAN TRICKED KING DAVID WITH ONE IN 2 SAMUEL 12, AND SEVERAL OF THE PROPHETS USED PARABLES.

So how did people react to Jesus' parables?

THE REACTIONS WERE A BIT MIXED. SOME OF JESUS' PARABLES WERE UNDERSTOOD STRAIGHT AWAY. EVEN HIS ENEMIES GOT THE POINT...

> The chief priests and the Pharisees heard Jesus' parables and knew that he was talking about them...
>
> MATTHEW 21:45

BUT ON OTHER OCCASIONS (ESPECIALLY MARK 8:14-21) THE THINGS JESUS SAID IN PICTURE-LANGUAGE BAFFLED EVEN HIS CLOSEST FOLLOWERS. THE PARABLE OF THE SOWER (MARK 4:1-20) WAS COMPLETELY BEYOND THEM. SO WHY DID JESUS USE PARABLES?

TO REVEAL

JESUS USED PARABLES PARTLY TO HELP PEOPLE UNDERSTAND AND FEEL FOR WHAT HE WAS SAYING. THE PARABLE OF THE GOOD SAMARITAN (LUKE 10:30-37), WHICH CRITICIZED JESUS' LISTENERS AND PRAISED THE SAMARITANS (WHOM THEY HATED) WOULD IMMEDIATELY HAVE COMMUNICATED AND SHOCKED THEM. GOD'S TRUTH WAS QUICKLY REVEALED.

TO CONCEAL

BUT JESUS ALSO USED PARABLES TO CONCEAL WHAT GOD WAS SAYING FROM THOSE WHO HAD NO FAITH. THERE WERE TIMES WHEN JESUS WOULD NOT SPEAK OUT OPENLY - INSTEAD HE USED RIDDLES SO THAT ONLY THOSE WHO WERE REALLY SERIOUS WOULD UNDERSTAND HIM (SEE LUKE 8:9-10). THIS IS STILL TRUE FOR ANYONE TODAY WHO WISHES TO UNDERSTAND JESUS' PARABLES.

THE PHARISEES

Who were they?

Well, the word 'Pharisee' literally means 'the Separated Ones'. They saw themselves as a special, separate group, trying to keep God's laws. This aim was good, but they went wrong by looking down on the rest of the human race for not being as religious as they were.

THE PHARISEES FOLLOWED IN THE FOOTSTEPS OF EZRA IN THE OLD TESTAMENT. HE HAD STRESSED THE IMPORTANCE OF OBEYING GOD'S LAW, AND THE PHARISEES TRIED TO WORK THIS OUT IN MINUTE DETAIL. THEY DEVELOPED A GIGANTIC SYSTEM OF RULES THAT SPECIFIED <u>EXACTLY</u> WHAT YOU COULD AND COULDN'T DO. FOR EXAMPLE, THEY SAID THERE WERE THIRTY-NINE MAIN TYPES OF ACTS THAT YOU COULDN'T DO ON THE SABBATH (THE JEWISH DAY OF REST). THIS LED THEM TO SOME VERY PRECISE RULES...

Do not set a broken arm or leg on the Sabbath.

Do not cut your fingernails on the Sabbath.

Do not carry any burden on the Sabbath.

Believe it or not

THERE WAS ONE GROUP OF PHARISEES WHO OUTDID ALL THE REST FOR STRICTNESS. THEY WERE NICKNAMED 'THE BLEEDING PHARISEES'. APPARENTLY, THEY WERE SO DETERMINED NEVER TO COMMIT A SINGLE SIN THAT THEY WALKED AROUND WITH THEIR EYES CLOSED...

Don't cough on the Sabbath, don't blow your nose on the Sabbath...

Forget it!

WHAT DID JESUS THINK OF THE PHARISEES?

TEACH YOURSELF PHARISAISM

JESUS RECOGNIZED THAT THE PHARISEES WERE TRYING TO OBEY GOD. IN FACT, SOME OF HIS BEST FRIENDS WERE PHARISEES. BUT JESUS FELL OUT WITH THEM IN AT LEAST THREE WAYS —

1 JESUS AND THE PHARISEES DISAGREED ABOUT THE SABBATH. HE HEALED PEOPLE ON THE SABBATH, WHICH THE PHARISEES SAW AS UNLAWFUL WORK. THEY WERE FURIOUS, BUT JESUS SAID THAT HUMAN NEED MUST COME BEFORE RULES AND REGULATIONS.

2 THE PHARISEES WERE EXTREMELY PROUD OF THEIR RELIGIOUS TRADITIONS. BUT JESUS IGNORED THEM AND WENT STRAIGHT BACK TO WHAT THE OLD TESTAMENT SAID. HIS ATTITUDE DEEPLY OFFENDED AND ANGERED THE PHARISEES.

3 JESUS FINALLY ATTACKED THE PHARISEES FOR THEIR LACK OF LOVE TOWARDS THE PEOPLE. THEY DEMANDED THAT PEOPLE SHOULD KEEP THEIR RULES — BUT GAVE THEM NO HELP TO DO IT. JESUS' PUBLIC ATTACKS ON THE PHARISEES (SEE MATTHEW 23) HUMILIATED THEM IN FRONT OF EVERYONE. THEY WERE SOON OUT FOR REVENGE...

MARK 3:6 TELLS US THAT THE PHARISEES AND OTHERS GOT TOGETHER AND BEGAN TO PLOT TO HAVE HIM PUT TO DEATH.

SADDUCEES

THE SADDUCEES WERE ANOTHER RELIGIOUS GROUP WHO APPEAR IN THE GOSPELS. WHILE THE PHARISEES WERE MAINLY DRAWN FROM THE POORER SIDE OF SOCIETY, THE SADDUCEES WERE A RICH, RATHER ARROGANT GROUP OF ARISTOCRATS. IN JESUS' TIME THEY CONTROLLED THE SANHEDRIN (JEWISH COUNCIL).

THE SADDUCEES DISAGREED WITH THE PHARISEES ABOUT LIFE AFTER DEATH. THE SADDUCEES DIDN'T BELIEVE IN A RESURRECTION...

That was why they were so sad, you see.

© Ancient Jokes Inc.

109

John

AS SOON AS YOU OPEN JOHN'S GOSPEL, YOU DISCOVER THAT IT IS VERY DIFFERENT FROM MATTHEW, MARK AND LUKE...

Where have all of Jesus' great parables gone?

There aren't as many miracles!

Jesus seems to talk much more about himself!

Jesus gives long speeches rather than short, snappy sayings

Jesus is in Jerusalem a lot of the time

What is going on??

JOHN'S GOSPEL DOESN'T ATTEMPT TO TELL ALL THE DETAILS IN THE STORY OF JESUS. SO IF YOU WANT A COMPREHENSIVE ACCOUNT OF HIS LIFE, READ LUKE! INSTEAD, THE WRITER SAT DOWN AND WROTE IN ORDER TO DRAW OUT THE DEEP MEANING OF JESUS' LIFE. OF COURSE, HE GIVES ACCURATE DETAILS OF WHAT HAPPENED, BUT HIS OVERALL AIM WAS TO EXPLAIN WHAT IT ALL MEANT.

So that's why it's different from the other Gospels?

EXACTLY. JOHN PROBABLY WROTE HIS BOOK LATER THAN MATTHEW, MARK AND LUKE. TO FOLLOW IT, IT HELPS TO KNOW THE STORY OF JESUS' LIFE FROM THE OTHER GOSPELS.

How it Works

- JOHN 1:1-18 JESUS AS THE WORD OF GOD, WHO BECOMES A HUMAN BEING
- JOHN 1:19-51 THE WORK OF JOHN THE BAPTIST
- JOHN 2-12 JESUS' PUBLIC MINISTRY. JESUS DOES MANY 'SIGNS' WHICH CLEARLY POINT TO HIM AS THE SON OF GOD. HE DECLARES HIS IDENTITY OPENLY
- JOHN 13-17 AT THE LAST SUPPER, JESUS SPEAKS AT LENGTH TO HIS DISCIPLES
- JOHN 18-19 JESUS IS ARRESTED, TRIED AND CRUCIFIED
- JOHN 20-21 RESURRECTION APPEARANCES

IN JOHN'S GOSPEL, JESUS OPENLY DECLARES WHO HE IS. THERE ARE SEVEN SAYINGS OF JESUS IN THE BOOK THAT BEGIN WITH THE WORDS: 'I AM...'. EACH OF THESE SAYINGS GIVES US A DIFFERENT PICTURE OF JESUS' IDENTITY, AND THEY HELP US TO UNDERSTAND HIM. SO HERE THEY ARE...

66 I am the bread of life. He who comes to me will never go hungry, and he who believes in me will never be thirsty. **99** JOHN 6:35

66 I am the light of the world. Whoever follows me will never walk in darkness, but will have the light of life. **99** JOHN 8:12

66 I am the gate for the sheep. **99** JOHN 10:7

66 I am the good shepherd. The good shepherd lays down his life for the sheep. **99** JOHN 10:11

66 I am the resurrection and the life. He who believes in me will live, even though he dies; and whoever lives and believes in me will never die. **99** JOHN 11:25-26

66 I am the way and the truth and the life. **99** JOHN 14:6

66 I am the vine and my Father is the gardener. **99** JOHN 15:1

THE FATHER

IN JOHN, JESUS GIVES THE FULLEST TEACHING ABOUT HIS RELATIONSHIP TO GOD THE FATHER TO BE FOUND IN THE FOUR GOSPELS. HE SAYS THAT HE WAS SENT BY THE FATHER, THAT HE IS THE ONLY WAY TO THE FATHER, AND (MOST SHOCKING OF ALL TO HIS LISTENERS) THAT HE AND THE FATHER ARE ONE (JOHN 10:30). THESE PASSAGES IN JOHN WERE LATER CRUCIAL TO THE CHURCH IN FORMULATING BELIEF IN GOD AS A TRINITY.

WHY WAS JOHN'S GOSPEL WRITTEN? TOWARDS THE END OF THE BOOK, THE WRITER SEEMS TO ANSWER THIS:

THESE THINGS ARE WRITTEN THAT YOU MAY BELIEVE THAT JESUS IS THE CHRIST, THE SON OF GOD, AND THAT BY BELIEVING YOU MAY HAVE LIFE IN HIS NAME.
JOHN 20:31

PILATE

HEROD

Pontius Pilate – who was he?

HE WAS PROCURATOR OF JUDEA (A PROVINCE OF THE ROMAN EMPIRE). JUDEA WAS A VIOLENT AND DIFFICULT PLACE TO GOVERN, AND PILATE OFTEN USED HIS POWERS TO HAVE REBELS PUT TO DEATH.

THE CRUCIFIXION

PILATE IS BEST KNOWN TO HISTORY AS THE MAN WHO SENTENCED JESUS TO DEATH. IN THE GOSPELS HE COMES ACROSS AS A WEAK CHARACTER, EASILY SWAYED. HE BELIEVED IN JESUS' INNOCENCE, BUT HE DIDN'T WANT A RIOT. HE AGREED JESUS' DEATH WHEN THE CROWD SHOUTED...

If you let this man go, you are no friend of Caesar!

JOHN 19:12

HE DIDN'T WANT BAD REPORTS GETTING BACK TO HIS MASTERS IN ROME. BUT HE HAD HIS REVENGE ON THE JEWS BY PUTTING THESE WORDS ON JESUS' CROSS –

THE HEROD WHO RULED DURING THE MINISTRY OF JESUS WAS HEROD ANTIPAS, SON OF THE HEROD WHO TRIED TO KILL JESUS AS A BABY. HE WAS RULER OF GALILEE. LIKE MOST OF THE HERODS, ANTIPAS WAS AN UNSTABLE, VIOLENT MAN – AND HE WAS ALSO SUPERSTITIOUS (SEE MARK 6:16).

Herod Antipas comes into the story of Jesus at two important points –

1 HEROD HAD JOHN THE BAPTIST ARRESTED BECAUSE JOHN HAD CRITICIZED HIM FOR MARRYING HIS BROTHER'S WIFE. EVENTUALLY HEROD HAD JOHN PUT TO DEATH (MARK 6:14-29).

2 HEROD ALSO COMES INTO THE STORY AT JESUS' TRIAL (LUKE 23:6-12). PILATE HAD OFFENDED HEROD A YEAR OR TWO EARLIER BY PUTTING SOME GALILEANS (HEROD'S SUBJECTS) TO DEATH WITHOUT CONSULTING HIM. SO HE SENT JESUS TO HIM AS A DIPLOMATIC GESTURE (JESUS BEING FROM GALILEE). HEROD WAS DELIGHTED AS HE WANTED TO SEE A MIRACLE OR TWO. BUT JESUS REFUSED EVEN TO SPEAK TO HIM. HEROD SENT HIM BACK TO PILATE DRESSED AS A KING.

That Fox

JESUS' DESCRIPTION OF HEROD IN LUKE 13:32

112

Judas

THE RELIGIOUS LEADERS OF ISRAEL, WHO HATED JESUS, HAD A PROBLEM. THEY WANTED TO ARREST JESUS AND PUT HIM TO DEATH, BUT WERE AFRAID TO DO IT OPENLY AS JESUS WAS SO POPULAR. AND WITH UP TO 100,000 PILGRIMS CAMPING OUT AROUND JERUSALEM BY NIGHT (THEY WERE THERE FOR THE PASSOVER FESTIVAL) IT WAS IMPOSSIBLE TO FIND WHERE HE SLEPT TO ARREST HIM SECRETLY.

THE ANSWER TO THIS DIFFICULT PROBLEM WAS JUDAS — ONE OF JESUS' TWELVE DISCIPLES. HE WENT TO THE PLOTTING PRIESTS ONE DAY AND OFFERED HIS SERVICES...

What will you give me if I betray Jesus to you?

MATTHEW 26:15

I've never really understood why Judas betrayed Jesus. What was in it for him?

JUDAS AGREED TO ACT AS A TOUR GUIDE ON A MISSION OF DEATH.

THE SIMPLE ANSWER IS THAT HE DID IT FOR THE MONEY. HE LOOKED AFTER THE DISCIPLES' MONEY-BAG AND WAS KNOWN TO STEAL FROM IT (JOHN 12:6).

ANOTHER THEORY IS THAT HE WAS AFRAID OF WHAT THE AUTHORITIES MIGHT DO TO JESUS AND HIS FOLLOWERS. SO HE TRIED TO CLEAR HIS NAME BY SELLING JESUS TO THEM.

ANOTHER IS THAT JUDAS HAD ALWAYS SEEN JESUS AS THE POLITICAL MESSIAH (PAGE 101). BUT WHEN JESUS REFUSED TO FIT THIS DESCRIPTION, JUDAS BROUGHT MATTERS TO BOILING POINT IN HIS OWN WAY TO FORCE JESUS TO DECLARE HIMSELF. HE COMMITTED SUICIDE WHEN IT ALL WENT BADLY WRONG.

Judas's Footsteps

WHAT JUDAS DID IN THE FINAL DAYS OF JESUS' LIFE:

■ ANGRY AT JESUS BEING ANOINTED IN BETHANY JOHN 12:1-8

■ AGREES A PRICE TO BETRAY JESUS MATTHEW 26:14-16

■ JESUS PREDICTS WHAT JUDAS WILL DO JOHN 13:21-30

■ BETRAYS JESUS WITH A KISS MATTHEW 26:47-50

■ COMMITS SUICIDE MATTHEW 27:3-10

THE FINAL VERDICT OF THE FIRST CHRISTIANS ON JUDAS...

... Judas, who left to go to the place where he belongs.

ACTS 1:25

ACTS

THE BOOK OF ACTS WAS WRITTEN BY LUKE AS PART TWO OF THE STORY OF JESUS' GOOD NEWS. IT BEGINS WITH THE SAME EVENT THAT ENDS LUKE'S GOSPEL: JESUS' ASCENSION INTO HEAVEN. AT THAT EVENT, JESUS SAYS THESE WORDS...

> When the Holy Spirit comes upon you, you will be filled with power, and you will be witnesses for me in Jerusalem, in all Judea and Samaria, and to the ends of the earth.
>
> ACTS 1:8

THE REST OF THE BOOK FOLLOWS THE APOSTLES' PROGRESS AS THEY TOOK THE GOOD NEWS OF JESUS OUT INTO THE WORLD. IT ALL STARTED EARLY ONE MORNING IN JERUSALEM...

Jerusalem

TEN DAYS AFTER JESUS FINALLY LEFT HIS DISCIPLES, THE HOLY SPIRIT FELL ON THEM AND GAVE THEM THE POWER TO SPEAK TO THE PILGRIMS (ATTENDING A FEAST IN JERUSALEM) IN THEIR NATIVE LANGUAGES. PETER PREACHED AND 3,000 PEOPLE BECAME CHRISTIANS. THE CHURCH WAS BORN (ACTS 2).

Judea & Samaria

THE BELIEVERS STAYED IN JERUSALEM UNTIL THE EXECUTION OF STEPHEN, A CHURCH LEADER. A VIOLENT WAVE OF PERSECUTION FOLLOWED, FORCING CHRISTIANS TO FLEE OUT INTO PALESTINE (ACTS 8). BUT THIS HAD A POSITIVE EFFECT — EVERYWHERE THEY WENT THEY PREACHED THE GOOD NEWS. FOR THE FIRST TIME, THE MESSAGE WAS RECEIVED BY NON-JEWS.

- PHILIP PREACHES IN SAMARIA ACTS 8:4-25
- PHILIP ON THE GAZA ROAD ACTS 8:26-40
- PETER PREACHES IN JOPPA ACTS 9:32-43
- PETER AND THE CONVERSION OF CORNELIUS ACTS 10

Ends of the Earth

"What was it that made them want to go that far?"

WELL, IN ACTS 9 LUKE RECORDS THE CONVERSION STORY OF ALL TIME. SAUL (SOON TO BE CALLED PAUL) WAS A YOUNG PHARISEE WHO WAS CRUELLY PERSECUTING THE CHURCH. ON THE WAY TO DAMASCUS, WITH PERSECUTION IN MIND, HE UNEXPECTEDLY MET THE RISEN JESUS. HIS LIFE WAS COMPLETELY CHANGED. BY ACTS 13, SAUL AND HIS COMPANION BARNABAS WERE SENT OUT FROM ANTIOCH BY THE HOLY SPIRIT TO PREACH IN WHAT IS NOW TURKEY. IT WAS THE START OF THE JOURNEY TO THE ENDS OF THE EARTH.

TWO THEMES COME ACROSS POWERFULLY IN ACTS...

1 THE HOLY SPIRIT

EACH NEW BREAK-THROUGH IN THE CHURCH'S MISSION CAME THROUGH THE ACTIVITY OF THE SPIRIT, AS HE...

- GUIDED THE EARLY CHURCH ACTS 2-7
- LED PETER TO CORNELIUS ACTS 10:19-21
- PROMPTED SAUL ON HIS FIRST JOURNEY ACTS 13:2
- SENT PAUL INTO EUROPE ACTS 16:6-10
- ORDERED PAUL TO JERUSALEM ACTS 20:22

2 THE GENTILES

AT THE BEGINNING OF ACTS, THE CHRISTIAN FAITH APPEARED TO BE JUST ANOTHER JEWISH SECT. BUT BY THE END, IT WAS WELL ON THE WAY TO BEING AN INTERNATIONAL FAITH THAT COULD SPEAK TO THE WHOLE WORLD. THIS CHANGE ONLY HAPPENED BECAUSE GENTILES (NON-JEWS) WERE ADMITTED TO THE CHURCH WITHOUT FIRST HAVING TO BECOME JEWS.

IT STARTED WITH THE CONVERSION OF CORNELIUS, A ROMAN CENTURION. THEN SAUL WAS APPOINTED 'APOSTLE TO THE GENTILES' AT HIS CONVERSION. BOTH OF THESE KEY EVENTS ARE REPEATED THREE TIMES THROUGHOUT ACTS. REPEATING EVENTS IN THIS WAY SHOWED THEIR VITAL IMPORTANCE IN ANY EASTERN BOOK.

The End?

LUKE'S BOOK ENDS UP (AFTER AN EXCITING STORM AT SEA IN ACTS 27) WITH PAUL UNDER HOUSE ARREST IN ROME, AWAITING TRIAL. LOOKED AT ANOTHER WAY, IT ENDS WITH THE GOOD NEWS BEING PREACHED ON THE STREETS OF ROME, THE HEART OF THE EMPIRE. IT WAS ONLY THE BEGINNING...

PETER

> What was Peter like?

SIMON PETER WAS QUITE A CHARACTER. HE WAS A FISHERMAN WITH HIS BROTHER ANDREW ON THE SEA OF GALILEE. HE WAS MARRIED, HAD A STRONG NORTH COUNTRY ACCENT (MATTHEW 26:73), AND WAS WARM, QUICK AND IMPULSIVE BY NATURE. JESUS CALLED HIM TO BE ONE OF THE TWELVE DISCIPLES AND HE QUICKLY BECAME THE SPOKESMAN FOR THEM ALL. JESUS GAVE HIM THE NAME: 'THE ROCK'.

PETER'S FAITH, LIKE HIS TEMPERAMENT, COULD RISE TO THE HEIGHTS AND SINK TO THE DEPTHS (SOMETIMES IN THE SAME AFTERNOON). THESE QUOTES FROM JESUS SAY IT ALL...

> Blessed are you, Simon son of Jonah!

WHEN PETER CONFESSED JESUS TO BE THE SON OF GOD (MATTHEW 16:17)

HOWEVER...

> Out of my sight, Satan! You are a stumbling block to me!

AFTER PETER TRIED TO DISSUADE JESUS FROM GOING TO JERUSALEM TO DIE (MATTHEW 16:23)

PETER'S MERCURIAL FAITH WAS SOON TO BE SEVERELY TESTED.

CRISIS POINTS

THERE WERE TWO GREAT MOMENTS OF CRISIS IN PETER'S LIFE:

1 AT ONE POINT IN HIS MINISTRY, JESUS ASKED HIS DISCIPLES WHO THEY THOUGHT HE WAS. PETER SAID, 'THE MESSIAH, THE SON OF THE LIVING GOD' (SEE MATTHEW 16:13-20). JESUS APPOINTED PETER AS LEADER OF THE CHURCH, WHICH HE BECAME IN THE BOOK OF ACTS. THIS EVENT WAS FOLLOWED BY THE TRANSFIGURATION WHICH HAD A LASTING IMPACT ON PETER.

2 AFTER JESUS' ARREST, PETER, SCARED FOR HIS LIFE, DENIED THREE TIMES THAT HE KNEW JESUS (MARK 14:66-72). HIS LOYALTY WAS LATER TESTED BY JESUS THREE TIMES (JOHN 21:15-19), AND HE WAS FORGIVEN.

THE LETTERS

THIS SECTION CONTAINS THE BOOKS OF...

ROMANS, 1+2 CORINTHIANS, GALATIANS, EPHESIANS, PHILIPPIANS, COLOSSIANS, 1+2 THESSALONIANS, 1+2 TIMOTHY, TITUS, PHILEMON, HEBREWS, JAMES, 1+2 PETER, 1, 2 +3 JOHN, AND JUDE

THE LETTERS

OVER ONE THIRD OF THE NEW TESTAMENT CONTAINS THE MAIL OF THE EARLY CHURCH. TWENTY-ONE LETTERS ARE INCLUDED, WRITTEN BY VARIOUS CHRISTIAN LEADERS TO CHURCHES AND INDIVIDUALS IN THE YEARS FOLLOWING THE DEATH OF JESUS. THEY COVER A VAST RANGE OF SUBJECTS, BUT THEIR MAIN CONCERNS ARE TO EXPLAIN WHAT THE CHRISTIAN GOOD NEWS IS AND HOW IT CAN BE PUT INTO ACTION.

This may sound stupid, but...

Why are the letters in the New Testament anyway? Isn't it enough just to have the story of Jesus in Matthew, Mark, Luke and John?

NO, IT'S NOT ENOUGH. ALTHOUGH THE GOSPELS TELL US A LOT ABOUT WHO JESUS WAS AND WHY HE CAME, THE LETTERS FILL OUT THE CHRISTIAN MESSAGE IN GREAT DETAIL. THEY ALSO SPELL OUT WHAT IT MEANS TO BE A CHRISTIAN.

So what drove them all to write these letters?

WELL, PAUL AND THE OTHERS DIDN'T JUST SIT DOWN ONE DAY AND DECIDE IT WOULD BE A NICE IDEA TO WRITE SOME LETTERS. THE LETTERS WEREN'T ISSUED FROM SOME IVORY TOWER, EITHER. INSTEAD, THEY WERE WRITTEN ON THE MOVE, IN THE MIDDLE OF REAL LIFE. AND THERE WERE DEFINITE REASONS FOR WRITING...

- TO COMBAT HERESY AND WRONG IDEAS (GALATIANS, COLOSSIANS)
- TO TACKLE CRISES THAT HAD ARISEN IN CHURCHES (1+2 CORINTHIANS)
- TO GIVE VITAL TEACHING (ROMANS, HEBREWS)
- TO GIVE ENCOURAGEMENT (1 PETER, 1 THESSALONIANS)
- PERSONAL (PHILEMON, 3 JOHN)

AFTER JESUS HIMSELF, PAUL IS THE DOMINANT FIGURE OF THE NEW TESTAMENT. HE WASN'T ONE OF JESUS' TWELVE DISCIPLES, AND IN FACT ACTIVELY TRIED TO DESTROY THE YOUNG CHRISTIAN FAITH. BUT HE WAS DRAMATICALLY CONVERTED (SEE PAGE 127) AND BECAME THE 'APOSTLE TO THE GENTILES'. PAUL WAS AN AMBITIOUS PIONEER. HIS JOURNEYS (INTO WHAT ARE NOW TURKEY, GREECE, ITALY AND SPAIN) ESTABLISHED CHURCHES IN PLACES THE FIRST FOLLOWERS OF JESUS WOULDN'T HAVE DREAMED ABOUT. HIS THIRTEEN NEW TESTAMENT LETTERS WERE VERY MUCH NEEDED BY THE ADOLESCENT CHURCHES AS THEY STRUGGLED TO GROW UP IN A HOSTILE WORLD.

PAUL'S LETTERS FALL INTO FOUR DIFFERENT SACKS...

THESE ARE THE EARLIEST OF PAUL'S LETTERS

THESE LETTERS EMPHASIZE THE MESSAGE OF PAUL

PAUL WROTE THESE LETTERS FROM PRISON

PAUL'S LAST ONES (ALSO CALLED 'THE PASTORAL LETTERS')

ROMANS

ROMANS IS ONE OF THE MAJOR BOOKS OF THE BIBLE. IT'S THE LONGEST OF PAUL'S LETTERS, AND IN IT HE GOES RIGHT TO THE HEART OF THE CHRISTIAN FAITH, EXPLAINING WHY JESUS DIED, AND HOW HIS DEATH CAN CHANGE PEOPLE. THROUGH HISTORY, ROMANS HAS HAD A POWERFUL EFFECT ON PEOPLE WHO WENT ON TO INFLUENCE THE WORLD OF THEIR TIME. FOR EXAMPLE...

MARTIN LUTHER WAS THE FATHER OF THE REFORMATION. HE STRUGGLED WITH HIS OWN SENSE OF GUILT BEFORE GOD UNTIL HE READ ROMANS. AND THEN —

> I felt myself to have been reborn and to have gone through open doors into paradise. The whole of Scripture took on a new meaning...

WRITTEN 1515

JOHN HESLEY, THE FOUNDER OF METHODISM, HAD A SIMILAR EXPERIENCE WITH ROMANS. IN HIS JOURNAL, HE DESCRIBES HOW HE WAS AT A MEETING WHERE SOMEONE WAS READING FROM A BOOK ON ROMANS WRITTEN BY MARTIN LUTHER —

> ...while he was describing the change which God works in the heart through faith in Christ, I felt my heart strangely warmed. I felt I did trust in Christ, Christ alone, for my salvation...

21 MAY 1738

BEWARE! BEFORE YOU PLUNGE IN AND READ ROMANS, JUST REMEMBER THAT IT'S HAD THE TENDENCY TO CHANGE PEOPLE'S LIVES DRASTICALLY. YOU HAVE BEEN WARNED...

THE BOOK OF ROMANS WAS WRITTEN AROUND AD 55. PAUL WAS STAYING IN THE CITY OF CORINTH AT THE TIME. HE WROTE TOWARDS THE END OF HIS LIFE, WHEN HE WAS AT THE HEIGHT OF HIS POWERS. ROMANS IS THEREFORE MATURE PAUL. IT'S HIS LIFETIME'S REFLECTION ON WHAT THE CHRISTIAN FAITH REALLY IS.

But _why_ did he write it?

FOR AGES PAUL HAD WANTED TO VISIT THE CHRISTIANS IN ROME. IT NOW LOOKED AS IF, AT LAST, HE WOULD BE ABLE TO MAKE THE JOURNEY TO SEE THEM. SO HE WROTE TO THESE PEOPLE HE HAD NOT YET MET, TO INTRODUCE HIS MESSAGE TO THEM. IN HIS LETTER HE COVERS THE WHOLE OF CHRISTIAN EXPERIENCE, AND HE RANGES FROM TREMENDOUSLY DEEP THOUGHTS TO THE PRACTICAL SIDE OF LIVING IT OUT.

THIS IS HOW THE LETTER LOOKS IN DETAIL...

1. OUR NEED
PAUL SHOWS HOW ALL PEOPLE ARE GUILTY BEFORE GOD

2. GOD'S ANSWER
GOD PUTS US RIGHT WITH HIM THROUGH JESUS CHRIST

3. NEW LIFE
HERE PAUL SHOWS WHAT IT MEANS TO BE A CHRISTIAN

The Christian Church, Near the Colisum, ROME, West Mea.

ROMANS 1:18 - 3:20

ROMANS 3:21 - 4:25

ROMANS 5 - 8

ROMANS 9 - 11

ROMANS 12:1 - 15:13

5. INTO ACTION
THESE CHAPTERS DEAL WITH CHRISTIAN LIVING ON AN EVERYDAY LEVEL

4. THE JEWS
PAUL LOOKS AT HOW ALL THIS AFFECTS THE JEWISH PEOPLE

NOW TRY

READING IT

FOR YOURSELF...

1 Corinthians

1 CORINTHIANS IS A LETTER WRITTEN BY PAUL TO THE MOST STORMY CHURCH OF NEW TESTAMENT TIMES. THE CHURCH WAS BEING TORN APART BY VICIOUS ARGUMENTS, IMMORALITY AND QUARRELLING GROUPS. THE SITUATION WAS ALMOST OUT OF CONTROL, AND PAUL'S LETTER IS AN ATTEMPT AT FIRE-FIGHTING.

The story so far...

IN THE FALL OF AD 50, PAUL ARRIVED IN CORINTH. HE WAS THE FIRST CHRISTIAN EVER TO SET FOOT IN THE CITY. HE STAYED EIGHTEEN MONTHS AND QUICKLY ESTABLISHED A CHURCH THERE. ACTS 18:1-17 DESCRIBES THIS VISIT IN DETAIL.

> But why did he stay so long?

BECAUSE CORINTH WAS ONE OF THE GREAT FOCUSES OF THE ROMAN EMPIRE. ALL THE MAIN EAST-WEST TRADE ROUTES PASSED THROUGH CORINTH, SO IT WAS ALWAYS FULL OF PEOPLE ON THE MOVE. IT WAS ALSO A NATURAL STOPPING-OFF POINT FOR TIRED BUSINESSMEN SEEKING A LITTLE RELAXATION. BECAUSE OF THIS, CORINTH WAS INFAMOUS FOR ITS ABYSSMALLY LOW MORAL STANDARDS. PAUL TOOK TIME TO ESTABLISH A CHURCH THERE SO THAT IT WOULD BE WELL-PROTECTED AGAINST THE PRESSURES AND TEMPTATIONS OF THE PAGANISM AROUND. BUT HE ALSO DID IT BECAUSE HE KNEW THAT A GREAT TRADING PLACE LIKE CORINTH COULD ALSO BECOME A PLACE FOR EXPORTING THE GOOD NEWS.

CITY LIMITS

ROMAN COLONY · FIRST CITY OF THE PROVINCE OF ACHAIA SINCE 27 BC

CORINTH
WELCOMES CAREFUL CHARIOTEERS

POPULATION 500,000

UNFORTUNATELY, DESPITE PAUL'S CAREFUL PREPARATION, THE YOUNG CHURCH QUICKLY DEVELOPED SERIOUS PROBLEMS.

The Christian Church,
22 Aphrodite Place,
CORINTH

SO PAUL SENT THEM A LETTER (THIS WAS BEFORE I CORINTHIANS). THIS LETTER NO LONGER EXISTS, BUT PAUL MENTIONS IT IN I CORINTHIANS 5:9. HE WARNS THEM TO STEER CLEAR OF MORALLY SUSPECT CHRISTIANS.

THEN TWO THINGS HAPPENED...

1 A SMALL NUMBER OF PEOPLE FROM CORINTH ARRIVED IN EPHESUS, WHERE PAUL WAS STAYING (I CORINTHIANS 1:11). THEY BROUGHT BAD NEWS ABOUT THE CHURCH...

- WARRING GROUPS WERE DEVELOPING
- A MAN HAD MARRIED HIS WIDOWED STEPMOTHER
- CHRISTIANS WERE TAKING EACH OTHER TO COURT
- THEIR MEETINGS HAD BECOME DRUNKEN FEASTS FOR RICH CHRISTIANS, WHILE POORER MEMBERS WENT HUNGRY

THIS WAY

So WHAT DID PAUL DO?

HE WROTE THEM A SECOND LETTER. THIS IS WHAT WE KNOW AS I CORINTHIANS.

2 ALMOST AT THE SAME TIME, A LETTER ARRIVED FROM THE CORINTHIANS THEMSELVES (I CORINTHIANS 7:1). THE LETTER (WHICH NO LONGER EXISTS) WAS FULL OF QUESTIONS LIKE THIS, ASKING PAUL'S ADVICE...

1/ How should Christians think about marriage, sex and divorce?
2/ Should we eat meat that's been used in pagan worship?
3/ How should women dress? And can they lead in the church?
4/ What about gifts from the Holy Spirit?
5/ What does this 'resurrection' mean? Surely the dead won't be raised to life?

URGENT   BY SHIP

The 'Apostle' Paul,
Near the Hall of Tyrannus,
EPHESUS

▌ I Corinthians

PAUL STARTED HIS LETTER (CHAPTERS 1-6) WITH THE REPORT HE HAD HEARD FROM THE SMALL GROUP OF PEOPLE. HE WROTE EXTREMELY STRONGLY, EVEN USING SARCASM TO POINT OUT THE TERRIBLE DANGER THEY WERE IN.

THEN FROM THE BEGINNING OF CHAPTER 7, HE STARTED TO ANSWER THE QUESTIONS IN THEIR LETTER TO HIM.

I CORINTHIANS, WRITTEN IN THE HEAT OF A DIFFICULT SITUATION, IS PRICELESS FOR THE CHRISTIAN TEACHING IT GIVES. IT IS BEST KNOWN FOR TWO GREAT PASSAGES: CHAPTER 13 (ON THE PRIME IMPORTANCE OF LOVE), AND CHAPTER 15 (ON THE RESURRECTION).

THE CORINTHIANS, THOUGH, TOOK IT BADLY. THE STORY CONTINUES ON PAGE 126.

PAUL The Writer

IT MAY COME AS A SURPRISE TO LEARN THAT PAUL DIDN'T WRITE HIS OWN LETTERS. INSTEAD, HE DICTATED WHAT HE HAD TO SAY TO AN **AMANUENSIS**, WHO WROTE IT ALL DOWN...

P.S. ACCORDING TO TRADITION, PAUL WAS SHORT, DARK AND BALDING...

Take a letter to the Philippians

Right!

THE AMANUENSIS ALSO HELPED TO PHRASE WHAT THE WRITER HAD TO SAY. ON ONE OCCASION, PAUL'S WRITER SIGNED HIMSELF OFF...

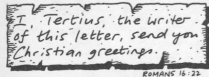

I, Tertius, the writer of this letter, send you Christian greetings.

ROMANS 16:22

AND AT OTHER TIMES PAUL HIMSELF GRABBED THE PEN TO FINISH A LETTER...

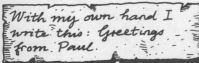

With my own hand I write this: Greetings from Paul.

COLOSSIANS 4:18

The Post

PAUL'S LETTERS WERE CARRIED BY FRIENDS TO THEIR DESTINATIONS. IT COULD TAKE SIX TO EIGHT WEEKS FOR A LETTER TO REACH PHILIPPI FROM ROME. AND A JOURNEY FROM ROME TO JERUSALEM TOOK JUST OVER THREE MONTHS, IF THE WEATHER WAS GOOD.

Couldn't they go any faster?

Yes – the Imperial Post took half the time!

ROMAN LETTERS OF THE FIRST CENTURY AD DIDN'T START 'DEAR...' THEY ALWAYS BEGAN WITH THE WRITER'S NAME, THEN THE READER'S, AND THEN A GREETING. LIKE THIS: 'ANTONY, TO CLEOPATRA: LOVE AND KISSES...' PAUL USED THE STANDARD ROMAN OPENING, BUT WITH A STRONG CHRISTIAN EMPHASIS.

PAUL'S NEW TESTAMENT LETTERS WEREN'T JUST PRIVATE AFFAIRS – THEY WERE MEANT TO BE READ OUT TO THE WHOLE CHURCH (1 THESSALONIANS 5:27).

PAUL

PAUL COULDN'T HAVE PICKED A BETTER TIME, IN THE ANCIENT WORLD, TO HAVE DONE HIS EXTENSIVE TRAVELLING. THERE WERE A LOT OF FACTORS THAT MADE TRAVEL IN THE ROMAN WORLD EASY. THERE WAS PEACE THROUGHOUT THE EMPIRE. FRONTIERS WERE QUITE EASY TO CROSS. THE SEAS WERE PIRATE-FREE. AND ROMAN ROADS WERE STRAIGHT, QUICK, AND WENT JUST ABOUT EVERYWHERE.

BUT WHAT WAS IT LIKE TO TRAVEL THEN? ON THE ROAD, PAUL AND HIS COMPANIONS WOULD HAVE BEEN PASSED BY CHARIOTS CARRYING THE IMPERIAL POST, SLOWLY-MOVING PASSENGER COACHES, AND ELEGANT CARRIAGES FOR THE WEALTHY. PAUL HIMSELF PROBABLY TRAVELLED ON FOOT OR BY MULE, COVERING ABOUT 20 MILES/32 KMS EACH DAY.

All he lacked was wings!

Rome, here I come!

TRAVEL COULD BE VERY UNCOMFORTABLE. IN A RARE PASSAGE, PAUL MOANS ABOUT THE CONDITIONS...

66 In my many travels I have been in danger from floods and from robbers... I have often been without enough food, shelter or clothing. 99 2 CORINTHIANS 11:26,27

So where did they sleep at night?

PAUL WAS A TENT-MAKER BY TRADE (ACTS 18:3), SO HE MAY HAVE JOINED THE MANY PEOPLE WHO CAMPED BY THE SIDE OF THE ROAD AT NIGHT. THE INNS WERE THICK WITH THIEVES AND TOO DANGEROUS TO STAY IN. BUT BEST OF ALL WAS TO STAY WITH FRIENDS— PAUL WAS PROBABLY ABLE TO RELY A LOT ON THIS (SEE PHILEMON 22).

PAUL ALSO TRAVELLED BY SEA, USUALLY DURING THE SAFE SAILING SEASON (26 MAY TO 14 SEPTEMBER). HIS SHIPWRECK IN ACTS 27 (AN OCTOBER VOYAGE) IS ONE OF THE MOST EXCITING ACCOUNTS WE HAVE OF AN ANCIENT SHIPWRECK.

2 Corinthians

PAUL'S SECOND LETTER TO THE CHRISTIANS IN CORINTH IS THE FINAL EPISODE IN A LONG STORY. TO TAKE IT FROM THE BEGINNING, TURN BACK TO PAGE 122 AND START FROM 1 CORINTHIANS.

So what happened after Paul sent 1 Corinthians?

IT LOOKS LIKE PAUL'S LETTER WENT DOWN BADLY IN CORINTH. AS A RESULT, PAUL HAD TO MAKE A SHORT, EMERGENCY VISIT TO THEM FROM WHERE HE WAS STAYING IN EPHESUS, 300 MILES ACROSS THE AEGEAN SEA. PAUL HOPED TO SORT OUT THE PROBLEMS, BUT THE VISIT WAS UNPLEASANT AND PROVED TO BE A FAILURE. THE PROBLEMS OF QUARRELLING AND DIVISION IN THE CHURCH WERE AS BAD AS EVER.

SO PAUL WROTE <u>ANOTHER</u> LETTER (NO COPIES OF THIS HAVE SURVIVED — IT WAS WRITTEN IN BETWEEN 1 + 2 CORINTHIANS). THIS IS OFTEN CALLED PAUL'S 'SEVERE LETTER' (SEE 2 CORINTHIANS 2:4). PAUL HOPED THAT HIS HARSH WORDS WOULD SHOCK THE CORINTHIANS TO THEIR SENSES. ONE OF HIS TRUSTED WORKERS, TITUS, TOOK THIS LETTER TO CORINTH.

MEGA-URGENT
The Christian Church,
22 Aphrodite Place,
CORINTH
WARNING: sit down before reading this letter.

2 Corinthians

LIKE MOST PEOPLE WHO SEND DIFFICULT LETTERS, PAUL WAS ANXIOUS TO HEAR HOW HIS READERS WOULD REACT. HE HAD ARRANGED TO MEET TITUS TO GET THIS NEWS, AND WHEN THEY FINALLY MET UP, THE NEWS WAS GOOD. THE CORINTHIANS HAD TAKEN TO HEART WHAT PAUL HAD WRITTEN, AND HAD CHANGED THEIR WAYS (SEE 2 CORINTHIANS 2:12-13; 7:5-16). THE LETTER WE KNOW AS 2 CORINTHIANS WAS HIS JOYFUL RESPONSE TO THEM.

2 CORINTHIANS IS ONE OF PAUL'S MOST PERSONAL LETTERS AND REVEALS A LOT ABOUT HIS FEELINGS AS HE WENT THROUGH DOUBT, DISAPPOINTMENT AND (ULTIMATELY) TRIUMPH WITH THE CORINTHIAN CHRISTIANS.

PAUL

HIS CONVERSION

Do you know Paul the Apostle?

No – but if you hum it, I'll play along...

THE APOSTLE PAUL IS ONE OF THE GREAT PIONEERS OF THE NEW TESTAMENT. OVER HIS THIRTY-YEAR CAREER, HE TRAVELLED THE ROMAN EMPIRE, PREACHING THE GOOD NEWS, FOUNDING CHURCHES, SUFFERING PERSECUTION AND IMPRISONMENT, SETTLING DISPUTES, DEBATING WITH PHILOSOPHERS AND ENCOURAGING NEW CHRISTIANS. AND IN HIS SPARE TIME, WRITING THE LETTERS THAT MAKE UP THE BULK OF THE NEW TESTAMENT. BUT PAUL WASN'T ONE OF THE ORIGINAL TWELVE APOSTLES. SO WHO WAS HE?

> The man who used to persecute us is now preaching the faith he once tried to destroy!

HOW PAUL'S CONVERSION WAS TALKED ABOUT IN THE EARLY CHURCH (GALATIANS 1:23)

PAUL (KNOWN THEN AS SAUL) WAS A VICIOUS PERSECUTOR OF THE FIRST CHRISTIANS. HE WAS A PHARISEE, AND WAS GIVEN AUTHORITY TO ROOT OUT AND ARREST CHRISTIANS, AND HE VOTED TO HAVE SOME KILLED (ACTS 26:9-11). BUT IN ACTS 9 HE HAD A SHOCKING ENCOUNTER WITH THE RISEN JESUS WHILE TRAVELLING TO DAMASCUS ON YET ANOTHER 'SEEK AND DESTROY' MISSION. HE BECAME A CHRISTIAN AND IMMEDIATELY STARTED PREACHING THAT JESUS WAS THE SON OF GOD. THIS EVENT HAD AN IMPACT ON PAUL IN AT LEAST TWO WAYS...

- HE WAS COMPLETELY CONVINCED THAT HE HAD MET JESUS, ALIVE FROM THE DEAD.

- HE WAS ALSO CONVINCED THAT HE HAD BEEN CALLED AS AN APOSTLE (SEE 1 CORINTHIANS 15:8-10). HIS CALL WAS AS THE APOSTLE TO THE GENTILES (NON-JEWS), A CALL WHICH HE REMARKABLY FULFILLED.

PAUL PREACHED IN DAMASCUS FOR THREE YEARS, UNTIL HIS ENEMIES FORCED HIM TO ESCAPE BY NIGHT...

GALATIANS

SOME THIRTEEN YEARS AFTER JESUS' DEATH, PAUL BEGAN HIS FIRST PREACHING JOURNEY. HE AND BARNABAS HEADED INTO THE ROMAN PROVINCE OF GALATIA (NOW TURKEY). THEY PREACHED IN FOUR TOWNS, AND GROUPS OF CHRISTIANS WERE FORMED THERE (ACTS 13-14). THESE NEW CHRISTIANS CAME FROM BOTH JEWISH AND NON-JEWISH BACKGROUNDS.

So far, so good...

BUT WITHIN A FEW YEARS THERE WERE PROBLEMS AMONG THESE CHURCHES. IT SEEMS THAT SOME JEWISH CHRISTIANS ARRIVED AFTER PAUL HAD LEFT (THEY ARE KNOWN AS THE 'JUDAIZERS'). THEY CAUSED A LOT OF TROUBLE BY PREACHING A DIFFERENT MESSAGE FROM PAUL'S...

PAUL'S MESSAGE	JUDAIZERS' MESSAGE
TO BE A CHRISTIAN IS TO RECEIVE GOD'S GIFT OF NEW LIFE BY FAITH IN JESUS CHRIST.	TO BE A CHRISTIAN MEANS THAT YOU FIRST HAVE TO BECOME A JEW (IF YOU AREN'T ONE ALREADY). THEN YOU HAVE FAITH IN JESUS ON TOP OF THAT.

So why did these Judaizers believe that?

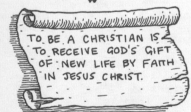

WELL, IT GOES BACK A LONG WAY. SINCE THE TIME OF MOSES, THE JEWS HAD BELIEVED THEY HAD BEEN SPECIALLY CHOSEN BY GOD TO BE HIS PEOPLE — AND THAT NO OTHER NATION HAD THE SAME PRIVILEGE. THEY THEREFORE DIVIDED THE WORLD IN TWO — THERE WERE JEWS, AND THERE WERE GENTILES.

THE OFFICIAL ATTITUDE TOWARDS GENTILES WAS THAT THE JEWS SHOULD TRY TO BRING THEM IN TO BECOME PART OF GOD'S PEOPLE. THIS DID HAPPEN, BUT SOMETIMES GENTILES WERE AVOIDED AND SEEN AS INFERIOR.

THIS WAY

So how did the coming of Jesus change all that?

The early church had to decide if the good news was for Jews only, or if it was for the whole human race. If it was only for Jews, then to become a Christian, you had first to become a Jew...

...WHICH MEANT CIRCUMCISION (IF YOU WERE A MAN!), OBSERVING THE JEWISH FEASTS, NOT EATING PORK, ETC. THIS IS EXACTLY WHAT THE JUDAIZERS INSISTED ON WHEN THEY ARRIVED IN GALATIA. PAUL'S GENTILE CONVERTS NOW HAD TO BECOME JEWS, AND HAD TO STRUGGLE TO KEEP ALL THE OLD TESTAMENT LAWS. WHEN PAUL HEARD ABOUT IT, HE WAS FURIOUS. HE DASHED OFF HIS LETTER TO THE GALATIANS TO SHOW THEM THAT THE JUDAIZERS WERE WRONG IN AT LEAST FOUR WAYS...

1 GALATIANS 2:21 PAUL SAID THAT IT WAS USELESS TRYING TO PLEASE GOD BY KEEPING ALL THE OLD TESTAMENT LAWS — NO ONE COULD EVER DO IT! THIS IS WHY JESUS CAME — TO OPEN UP A NEW WAY TO GOD. TO CLING TO THE OLD LAWS AS A WAY OF PUTTING THINGS RIGHT WITH GOD WAS TO DENY WHAT JESUS CAME TO DO.

2 GALATIANS 3:3 PAUL SAID THAT CHRISTIANS RECEIVED THEIR POWER FOR LIVING AS GOD WANTED FROM GOD'S SPIRIT. TO EXCHANGE THIS POWER FOR THEIR OWN WEAK WILLPOWER TO KEEP THE LAW WAS JUST STUPID!

3 GALATIANS 5:1 JESUS CAME TO FREE PEOPLE FROM THE SLAVERY THAT SIN AND GUILT BRINGS. BUT TO SUBMIT TO THE LAW MEANT THAT THE GALATIANS WERE BECOMING SLAVES AGAIN. THEY SHOULD LEARN TO VALUE THEIR FREEDOM.

4 GALATIANS 5:13 PAUL SOUNDS A WARNING NOTE: THIS CHRISTIAN FREEDOM IS FREEDOM TO DO GOOD, AND NOT A LICENCE TO BEHAVE BADLY. THIS IS THE POWER OF CHRIST'S GOOD NEWS. IT GIVES PEOPLE THE POWER TO LIVE AS GOD HAS ALWAYS INTENDED (SEE GALATIANS 5:22-23).

ephesians

EPHESUS WAS ONE OF THE GREAT CITIES OF THE ANCIENT WORLD. IT WAS AN IMPORTANT PORT WITH LINKS TO CORINTH AND ROME. IT HAD ITS OWN GODDESS, DIANA, WITH A TEMPLE FOUR TIMES BIGGER THAN THE PARTHENON IN ATHENS. IT HAD A THEATRE SEATING UP TO 50,000 PEOPLE ON A GOOD NIGHT. AND THE CITY BOASTED 1/3 MILLION PEOPLE.

THE APOSTLE PAUL CAME HERE AROUND AD 54 AND STAYED FOR OVER TWO YEARS...

Is there anywhere he didn't go?

ACTS 19 DESCRIBES PAUL'S TIME IN EPHESUS. HE MADE THE CITY THE HEADQUARTERS FOR HIS WORK IN ASIA MINOR (NOW CALLED TURKEY). BUT TOWARDS THE END OF HIS TIME IN EPHESUS, THERE WAS A RIOT STIRRED UP BY THE SELLERS OF RELIGIOUS SOUVENIRS. PAUL'S MESSAGE WAS EATING INTO THEIR TRADE! BUT THE RIOT WAS SO SERIOUS THAT PAUL LEFT TOWN WHEN IT WAS ALL OVER.

If Paul was in Ephesus that long, he must have known most of the Christians personally. Yet in this letter, he doesn't mention anyone by name. How do you explain that?

IT'S BELIEVED THAT EPHESIANS WAS WRITTEN NOT ONLY TO THE CHURCH IN EPHESUS, BUT TO A WHOLE GROUP OF CHURCHES IN THE AREA. EPHESUS WAS PROBABLY THE BIGGEST OF THESE CHURCHES AND MAY THEREFORE HAVE BEEN AT THE TOP OF THE LIST. ONCE THE EPHESIAN CHRISTIANS HAD READ IT, THE LETTER WOULD THEN HAVE BEEN SENT AROUND TO THE OTHER CHURCHES. THIS 'PASS IT ON' METHOD IS DESCRIBED IN COLOSSIANS 4:16.

So the letter wasn't just meant to be read by the Ephesians — which is just as well, because most of the millions of people who have read it haven't been Ephesians!

Mmm. So what's in it?

THIS WAY

PAUL STARTS IN CHAPTER 1 BY SHOWING THAT THE DEATH OF JESUS WASN'T JUST SOME ISOLATED EVENT IN THE BACKWATERS OF HISTORY. INSTEAD, JESUS' DEATH WAS THE KEY INGREDIENT IN GOD'S GREAT PLAN FOR HIS WHOLE CREATION. THIS PLAN WAS ON THE GRAND SCALE — TO REUNITE THE HUMAN RACE WITH HIMSELF, BY FORGIVING OUR SINS AND SETTING US FREE TO BE HIS CHILDREN. AS PAUL PUTS IT...

> This plan is to bring all creation together, everything in heaven and on earth, with Christ as head.

EPHESIANS 1:10

It all sounds a bit heavy to me...

WELL, READ ON, BECAUSE PAUL SPELLS OUT WHAT THIS MEANS IN THREE WAYS.

New Unity

THE DEATH OF JESUS REUNITES PEOPLE WITH GOD. IT ALSO REUNITES THEM WITH EACH OTHER, BREAKING DOWN THE WALLS WHICH DIVIDE PEOPLE (EPHESIANS 2:11-22). SO JEWS AND NON-JEWS, WHO USED TO BE TWO SEPARATE (AND SOMETIMES OPPOSED) GROUPS, NOW BECOME ONE IN CHRIST. SEE EPHESIANS 4:1-16.

1

New Life

2

THE DIFFERENCE BETWEEN LIVING WITHOUT GOD AND LIVING WITH GOD IS AS RADICAL AS THE DEAD COMING BACK TO LIFE (EPHESIANS 2:1-10). PAUL DETAILS THE DIFFERENCE THIS MAKES IN EPHESIANS 4:17 – 5:20. IT MEANS A COMPLETE BREAK WITH THE OLD WAY OF LIFE. IN A FAMOUS NEW TESTAMENT PASSAGE, PAUL COMPARES THE STRUGGLE TO LIVE IN THIS WAY TO A ROMAN SOLDIER PUTTING ON BATTLE-DRESS BEFORE A FIGHT (EPHESIANS 6:10-20).

3

New Relationships

THIS NEW WAY OF LIFE WORKS OUT CLEARLY IN RELATIONSHIPS. HUSBANDS AND WIVES, PARENTS AND CHILDREN, BOSSES AND WORKERS ALL HAVE TO RELATE IN A NEW WAY (EPHESIANS 5:21-6:9). AND THE NEW ATTITUDE IN ALL THIS IS TO 'SUBMIT TO ONE ANOTHER'.

Philippians

PHILIPPIANS IS ONE OF THE FOUR LETTERS IN THE NEW TESTAMENT WHICH PAUL WROTE FROM PRISON. THESE LETTERS ARE EPHESIANS, PHILIPPIANS, COLOSSIANS AND PHILEMON. TRADITIONALLY, IT'S BEEN BELIEVED THAT PAUL WROTE THESE LETTERS FROM HIS CAPTIVITY

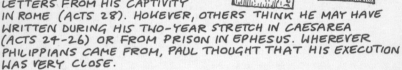

IN ROME (ACTS 28). HOWEVER, OTHERS THINK HE MAY HAVE WRITTEN DURING HIS TWO-YEAR STRETCH IN CAESAREA (ACTS 24-26) OR FROM PRISON IN EPHESUS. WHEREVER PHILIPPIANS CAME FROM, PAUL THOUGHT THAT HIS EXECUTION WAS VERY CLOSE.

> So why did he write to Philippi?

PAUL AND THE PHILIPPIANS WENT BACK A LONG WAY. RIGHT BACK TO AD 50 IN FACT, WHEN PAUL WAS ON HIS SECOND ROUND OF TRAVELLING. HE HADN'T INTENDED AT ALL TO GO TO PHILIPPI (WHICH WAS THE CHIEF CITY OF MACEDONIA). BUT ONE NIGHT HE HAD A VISION IN WHICH A MAN APPEARED TO HIM AND SAID...

> Come over to Macedonia and help us...
>
> ACTS 16:9

PAUL WENT STRAIGHT AWAY, AND SO THE GOOD NEWS REACHED EUROPE.

PAUL'S EARTH-SHAKING TIME IN PHILIPPI IS RECORDED IN ACTS 16:11-40. HE FORMED A CLOSE RELATIONSHIP WITH THE NEW CHURCH THERE, ESPECIALLY WHEN THEY LATER HELPED HIM THROUGH HARD TIMES (SEE PHILIPPIANS 4:15-16). HE WROTE TO THEM FOR SEVERAL REASONS:

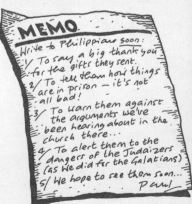

MEMO

Write to Philippians soon:
1/ To say a big thank you for the gifts they sent.
2/ To tell them how things are in prison — it's not all bad!
3/ To warn them against the arguments we've been hearing about in the church there...
4/ To alert them to the dangers of the Judaizers (as we did for the Galatians)
5/ We hope to see them soon...

Paul

"Are there any special passages to look out for?"

"Well, it's all pretty special, but here are three areas..."

2. PHILIPPIANS 2:6-11

PAUL QUOTES THIS ANCIENT SONG (EITHER WRITTEN BY HIMSELF OR BY ANOTHER OF THE FIRST CHRISTIANS). THE SONG IS A MAGNIFICENT AND YET SIMPLY-PUT DESCRIPTION OF THE HUMILIATION AND EXALTATION OF JESUS. PAUL USED IT HERE TO SHOW THAT THERE WAS NO ROOM FOR PRIDE AMONG CHRISTIANS.

1. PHILIPPIANS 1:20-26

HERE, PAUL IS TORN BETWEEN WANTING TO DIE (TO BE WITH CHRIST) OR CARRYING ON THE WORK GOD HAD GIVEN HIM TO DO IN THIS WORLD. THE PASSAGE GIVES AN INSIGHT INTO HOW ONE CHRISTIAN SAW HIS COMING DEATH.

3. PHILIPPIANS 3:1-11

PAUL ATTACKS THE FALSE TEACHERS WHO WANT CHRISTIANS TO SUBMIT TO JEWISH LAWS. HE WRITES OFF HIS OWN STRICT JEWISH PAST AS 'DUNG' (HE ACTUALLY USES A MUCH STRONGER WORD IN THE GREEK LANGUAGE) COMPARED TO KNOWING JESUS CHRIST.

Joy!

DESPITE THE FACT THAT PAUL WAS WRITING FROM A POTENTIAL DEATH-CELL, THE BACKBONE OF HIS LETTER IS JOY. HE WAS HAPPY TO SUFFER IF CHRIST WAS PREACHED. THE PHILIPPIANS KNEW ABOUT PAUL'S STUBBORN JOY FROM THE PAST...

About midnight, Paul and Silas were praying and singing hymns to God, and the other prisoners were listening to them...

IN THE PHILIPPI JAIL – ACTS 16:25

AND PAUL CALLS ON HIS READERS TO REJOICE WITH HIM – 'REJOICE IN THE LORD ALWAYS. I WILL SAY IT AGAIN: REJOICE!'

Finally...

PAUL SEEMS TO HAVE HAD A PROBLEM IN FINISHING OFF HIS LETTER. HE SAYS 'FINALLY...' TWICE, AND THE LETTER SEEMS TO FINISH A COUPLE OF TIMES, ONLY TO CARRY ON AGAIN! IS THIS WRITTEN EVIDENCE THAT PAUL WAS AS LONG-WINDED AS ACTS 20:7-12 SUGGESTS?

"AND FINALLY..."

COLOSSIANS

It probably all happened something like this...

PAUL WAS IN PRISON, PROBABLY IN ROME (SEE ACTS 28). ONE DAY, EPAPHRAS, A CONVERT OF PAUL'S AND TEACHER OF THE CHURCH IN COLOSSAE, ARRIVED IN ROME. HE SEARCHED FOR PAUL AND EVENTUALLY FOUND HIM. HE HAD BROUGHT GOOD AND BAD NEWS ABOUT THE CHRISTIANS IN COLOSSAE...

THIS WAY

PUT BRIEFLY, THE BAD REPORT EPAPHRAS BROUGHT WAS THIS...

To Paul
ERRORS AT COLOSSAE
(A) Some teachers are claiming that they have secret knowledge of salvation that is superior to Christian teaching.

(B) Jewish teachers want Christians to be circumcised, follow the food-laws, keep the festivals, etc...

(C) Others are emphasizing the power of the spirit-world more than the power of Jesus;
Help!   Epaphras

SO HOW DID PAUL RESPOND?

The good news?

THE COLOSSIAN CHURCH WAS STRONG AND STABLE.

And the bad?

A VARIETY OF ERRORS HAD CREPT IN. IT WAS THESE ERRORS WHICH HAD MADE EPAPHRAS TRAVEL THE 600 MILES TO SEE PAUL. AND THEY ALSO PROMPTED PAUL TO WRITE THIS LETTER TO COLOSSAE. HE WANTED TO STOP THE POISON.

PAUL RIGHTLY SAW THAT THESE TEACHINGS ATTACKED THE CENTRAL PLACE JESUS CHRIST HAS IN THE SALVATION OF THE HUMAN RACE. HE COUNTER-ATTACKED BY GIVING HIS FULLEST PIECE OF WRITING ON WHO JESUS IS AND WHAT HE CAME TO ACHIEVE...

God was pleased to have all his fullness dwell in him, and through him to reconcile to himself all things...

COLOSSIANS 1:19-20

TWO CHRISTIANS TOOK PAUL'S LETTER TO COLOSSAE (COLOSSIANS 4:7-9). ONESIMUS WAS A RUNAWAY SLAVE AND WAS PROBABLY ALSO CARRYING PAUL'S LETTER TO PHILEMON (SEE PAGE 143). TYCHICUS MAY WELL HAVE HAD PAUL'S LETTER TO THE EPHESIANS IN HIS POCKET AS WELL AS COLOSSIANS.

134

I Thessalonians

THESSALONICA WAS A MAJOR CITY AT THE TIME OF PAUL, AND IT STILL IS TODAY. IT STOOD ON ONE OF THE GREAT EAST-WEST ROMAN ROADS, AND WAS A NATURAL PLACE FOR PAUL TO VISIT.

So when did Paul go there?

ON HIS FIRST TRIP INTO GREECE, PAUL VISITED THESSALONICA AFTER HE HAD BEEN TO PHILIPPI AND SOME OTHER TOWNS. HIS TIME THERE IS DESCRIBED IN ACTS 17:1-9. PAUL'S MESSAGE (AS IT OFTEN DID) POLARIZED HIS HEARERS INTO TWO GROUPS — THOSE WHO WERE CONVINCED AND BELIEVED, AND OTHERS WHO WERE SCANDALIZED AND TOOK ACTION...

You became imitators of us and of the Lord; in spite of severe suffering, you welcomed the message with the joy given by the Holy Spirit.

THOSE WHO BELIEVED (PAUL IN 1 THESSALONIANS 1:6)

These men who have caused trouble all over the world have now come here!

THOSE WHO REJECTED (THE MOB IN ACTS 17:6)

MOB VIOLENCE FORCED PAUL TO LEAVE THE CITY BEFORE HE WAS READY. HE HADN'T FINISHED GIVING THE YOUNG CHURCH THE BASIC TEACHING IT NEEDED TO SURVIVE IN SUCH A HOSTILE PLACE. HE WENT ON TO ATHENS AND CORINTH, BUT TIMOTHY (PAUL'S APPRENTICE) WENT BACK TO THESSALONICA. HE SOON BROUGHT PAUL NEWS OF THE CHURCH THERE, WHICH PROMPTED PAUL TO WRITE THIS LETTER.

1/ Paul wrote partly to encourage the believers. The letter is warm and full of Paul's love and concern for his young converts.

2/ He also wrote to continue his teaching from where he had been forced to leave off. He covered moral living and the second coming of Christ.

SECRET
The Believers, c/o Jason's House THESSALONICA Macedonia

135

2 THESSALONIANS

THIS LETTER WAS PROBABLY SENT TO THE CHURCH IN
THESSALONICA SOON AFTER PAUL'S FIRST LETTER. HE
WROTE AGAIN BECAUSE HE HAD HEARD ABOUT SOME WRONG
IDEAS THAT HAD TAKEN ROOT IN THE CHURCH.

1 SOME OF THE THESSALONIANS WERE SAYING...

In his last letter, Paul told us that Jesus would return suddenly. Well, it's already started to happen!

THEIR CONFUSION OVER <u>WHEN</u>
CHRIST'S RETURN WOULD
HAPPEN MADE PAUL RESPOND
WITH SOME CLEAR TEACHING
ON EXACTLY <u>WHAT</u> THE
SECOND COMING WOULD INVOLVE.

PAUL SAID...

■ ...THAT BEFORE
CHRIST RETURNED THERE
WOULD BE A WORLD-WIDE
REBELLION AGAINST GOD.
THIS WOULD BE LED BY THE
MYSTERIOUS 'MAN OF
LAWLESSNESS'. BUT THIS
COULDN'T HAPPEN YET BECAUSE
A POWER FOR GOOD WAS
HOLDING EVIL IN CHECK
(2 THESSALONIANS 2:1-12).

■ ...THAT THE ACTUAL RETURN
OF CHRIST WOULD BE
CATACLYSMIC. HIS VIVID
DESCRIPTION OF WHAT IT
WOULD MEAN IS IN
2 THESSALONIANS 1:7-10.

2 THIS SAME GROUP WERE ALSO SAYING...

Well, if Christ is coming back so soon, there's no need to carry on working is there? We can just wait...

THEY THOUGHT THEY WERE
BEING HIGHLY SPIRITUAL. WORK
WAS TOO TRIVIAL WHEN THE
END OF THE WORLD WAS JUST
AROUND THE CORNER. BUT
PAUL CALLED THEM Lazy.

HE TOLD THEM THEY
SHOULD WORK IF THEY COULD.

I TIMOTHY

THIS FIRST LETTER TO TIMOTHY IS ONE OF THREE LETTERS PAUL WROTE AT THE END OF HIS LIFE. HE WAS CONCERNED ABOUT WHAT WOULD HAPPEN TO THE CHURCHES HE HAD CARED FOR OVER MANY YEARS. SO HE WROTE TO HIS TWO MOST TRUSTED ASSISTANTS, TIMOTHY AND TITUS, TO TELL THEM WHAT THEY SHOULD DO. I TIMOTHY WAS WRITTEN AFTER THE EVENTS DESCRIBED IN ACTS 28, WHEN PAUL HAD BEEN RELEASED FROM PRISON IN ROME.

THE 'PASTORAL' LETTERS

Fine. But who was this Timothy?

TIMOTHY WAS A YOUNG MAN (ALTHOUGH HE WAS PROBABLY OVER FORTY WHEN I TIMOTHY WAS WRITTEN!) WITH A JEWISH MOTHER AND A GREEK FATHER. TIMOTHY BECAME A CHRISTIAN WHEN PAUL VISITED HIS HOME TOWN (LYSTRA) ON HIS FIRST JOURNEY. THE NEXT TIME PAUL PASSED THROUGH THAT PART OF THE WORLD HE RECRUITED TIMOTHY TO JOIN THE TRAVELLING GROUP (ACTS 16:1-5). FROM THEN ON HE WAS A LOYAL WORKER FOR PAUL, AND HE IS MENTIONED FREQUENTLY AT THE END OF PAUL'S LETTERS. ACCORDING TO PAUL, TIMOTHY WAS A BIT TIMID, WHICH WAS WHY PAUL WROTE TO HIM WITH SUCH DIRECT INSTRUCTIONS.

I Timothy

I TIMOTHY CONCENTRATES ON THREE KEY AREAS:

- **CHAPTER 1** FALSE TEACHING. PAUL URGES TIMOTHY TO STAND FIRM.
- **CHAPTERS 2+3** LIFE IN THE CHURCH. PAUL TALKS ABOUT THE CHURCH'S WORSHIP AND ITS LEADERS.
- **CHAPTERS 4+5** TIMOTHY'S LEADERSHIP. PAUL FINALLY TURNS TO TIMOTHY WITH SOME PERSONAL WORDS.

ROMAN EMPIRE

Oh NO! Not the Roman Empire! It's all just dead history!

THE ROMAN EMPIRE MAY BE DEAD AND GONE, BUT IN THE TIME OF THE NEW TESTAMENT IT DOMINATED EVERYTHING. BY LOOKING AT HOW THE ROMANS RAN THE MEDITERRANEAN WORLD, WE GET A CLEARER PICTURE OF LIFE AS JESUS, PAUL AND THE REST EXPERIENCED IT.

ROME STARTED OFF AS A GROUP OF SMALL VILLAGES. EVENTUALLY THEY GREW INTO THE CITY. 750 YEARS LATER, WHEN JESUS WAS BORN, ROME RULED AN EMPIRE THAT TOOK IN ALL THE MEDITERRANEAN LANDS PLUS MODERN-DAY FRANCE, ENGLAND AND WALES. THE COUNTRIES CONQUERED BY ROME WERE KNOWN AS PROVINCES.

ROMAN EMPIRE (POCKET VERSION)

OKAY. THEN LOOK AT THIS. THE ROMAN EMPIRE WAS SO POWERFUL THAT ITS INFLUENCE IS STILL WITH US. FOR EXAMPLE...

History, history, history. Yawn!

❑ ROMAN LAW THE TWELVE TABLES AND THE JUSTINIAN CODE ARE STILL AT THE HEART OF WESTERN LAW.

❑ THE CALENDAR THE NAMES OF THE MONTHS, 1 JANUARY AS NEW YEAR'S DAY, THE 365-DAY YEAR — THEY ALL CAME FROM ROME.

❑ CITY-PLANS U.S. CITIES ARE LAID OUT ON A GRID PLAN, JUST AS ROMAN CITIES WERE...

❑ LATIN WAS THE LANGUAGE OF DIPLOMACY UNTIL THE 18th CENTURY. LATIN HAS HAD A POWERFUL INFLUENCE ON MANY MODERN LANGUAGES.

Judea

JUDEA (THE ROMAN NAME FOR THE LAND OF THE JEWISH PEOPLE) WAS A THIRD-RATE PROVINCE OF THE EMPIRE. ITS KINGS (THE HEROD FAMILY) WERE VIRTUALLY PUPPET RULERS. THE REAL POWER WAS IN ROME ITSELF, WHICH KEPT ORDER WITH THE ARMY.

> SO WHAT DID THE FIRST CHRISTIANS THINK OF THE ROMAN EMPIRE?

WELL, THEY SAW IT IN TWO WAYS...

GOOD

IN MANY WAYS THE ROMAN EMPIRE HELPED TO SPEED THE CHRISTIAN GOOD NEWS AROUND THE WORLD, BECAUSE OF:

- ROMAN ROADS, WHICH MADE TRAVEL QUITE QUICK.
- THE GREEK LANGUAGE, SPOKEN THROUGHOUT THE EMPIRE.
- THE PAX ROMANA (ROMAN PEACE) WHICH MEANT LIFE WAS STABLE AND SECURE.

SO THERE WAS A FRIENDLY ATTITUDE AMONG CHRISTIANS TO THE EMPIRE.

> Paul could even use images such as Roman battle-dress in his teaching

PAUL TOOK IT FURTHER AND SAID THAT AS GOD HAD GIVEN ROME ITS POWER, CHRISTIANS SHOULD OBEY THE STATE:

> Everyone must submit himself to the governing authorities, for there is no authority except that which God has established.
>
> ROMANS 13:1

BAD

ON THE OTHER HAND, CHRISTIANS COULD NEVER FORGET THAT IT WAS A ROMAN, PONTIUS PILATE, WHO HAD SENTENCED JESUS TO DEATH. AND AS THE MESSAGE SPREAD, ENEMIES OF THE CHRISTIANS ACCUSED THEM OF TREASON AGAINST THE EMPEROR:

> They are defying Caesar's decrees, saying that there is another king, one called Jesus.
>
> ACTS 17:7

CHRISTIANS ANSWERED THIS BY SAYING THAT THEY COULD WORSHIP JESUS AND OBEY THE EMPEROR. BUT THE CRUNCH CAME WHEN THEY WERE TOLD TO WORSHIP THE EMPEROR AS GOD INSTEAD OF JESUS. THIS HAPPENED IN THE REIGN OF DOMITIAN (FROM AD 81). PERSECUTION AND DEATH FOLLOWED FOR COUNTLESS CHRISTIANS.

THE BOOK OF REVELATION WAS WRITTEN AT THIS TIME OF PERSECUTION, AND EXPOSES ROME'S EVIL. ROME, LIKE ASSYRIA AND BABYLON IN THE OLD TESTAMENT, WOULD BE JUDGED AND DESTROYED BY GOD.

2 TIMOTHY

IT'S GENERALLY AGREED THAT THIS IS PAUL'S LAST LETTER...

Oh no! Is it going to be a weepie?

NO. PAUL'S LETTER CONTAINS WORDS OF THANKS, ENCOURAGEMENT, WARNINGS FOR THE FUTURE, HOPE, JOY, ETC. — BUT THERE'S NO SELF-PITY OR MOANING ABOUT HIS PREDICAMENT. PAUL WAS IN PRISON AGAIN IN ROME — THIS TIME FOR GOOD. HE KNEW THAT HIS EXECUTION WAS VERY NEAR (2 TIMOTHY 4:6).

WHY DID PAUL WRITE IT?

2 TIMOTHY IS ALMOST LIKE PAUL'S LAST WILL AND TESTAMENT. IN IT HE GIVES HIS FINAL WORDS TO TIMOTHY, HIS JUNIOR PARTNER IN THE FAITH, REMINDING HIM OF ALL THEY HAD BEEN THROUGH TOGETHER, AND TELLING HIM HOW TO ACT AS HIS SUCCESSOR. IT'S CLEAR FROM THE LETTER THAT PAUL WASN'T TOO SURE HOW TIMOTHY WOULD MEASURE UP TO HIS NEW RESPONSIBILITIES. SO HE REPEATEDLY TACKLES TIMOTHY'S WEAK NATURE (2 TIMOTHY 1:8, 2:1, ETC.). HE WAS GOING TO HAVE TO BE TOUGH TO TACKLE THE PROBLEMS FACING THE CHURCHES.
PAUL ALSO WRITES HIS OWN BEST EPITAPH AS HE SUMS UP THE FAITH HE HAD GIVEN HIS WHOLE LIFE TO... *THIS WAY*

final words

PAUL ENDS THE MIGHTY CORRESPONDENCE THAT DOMINATES THE NEW TESTAMENT WITH SOME TOUCHING PERSONAL DETAILS. SADLY, ONLY LUKE IS WITH HIM, WINTER IS COMING AND PAUL MISSES HIS BOOKS AND A WARM CLOAK HE LEFT BEHIND. HE ASKS TIMOTHY TO JOIN HIM QUICKLY. DID TIMOTHY EVER GET THERE IN TIME? NO ONE KNOWS...

I have fought the good fight, I have finished the race, I have kept the faith. Now there is in store for me the crown of righteousness, which the Lord, the righteous Judge, will award to me on that day...
2 TIMOTHY 4:7-8

TITUS

THE LETTER TO TITUS WAS WRITTEN BY PAUL TO ONE OF HIS CLOSE COMPANIONS ON CRETE. TITUS WAS HAVING A REALLY DIFFICULT TIME THERE. MANY OF THE CRETANS WERE HOT-HEADED AND OVERLY MACHO. THEY LOVED ARGUMENTS. THIS WAS TRUE EVEN OF THE CHURCH LEADERS —

> A church leader... must not be arrogant or quick-tempered, or a drunkard, or violent or greedy for money.
>
> TITUS 1:7

So how had Titus ended up with such a bunch in the first place?

PAUL HAD GONE WITH TITUS TO CRETE WHEN HE WAS SET FREE FROM THE IMPRISONMENT DESCRIBED IN ACTS 28. THEN PAUL LEFT HIM THERE TO LOOK AFTER THE YOUNG CHURCH, WHILE HE CARRIED ON TRAVELLING.

TITUS

TITUS HAD BEEN IN TWO HOT SITUATIONS BEFORE ON PAUL'S BEHALF...
- GALATIANS 2:1-5 HE WENT WITH PAUL AND BARNABAS ON A TRICKY VISIT TO THE JERUSALEM CHURCH.
- 2 CORINTHIANS 2:12-13; 7:5-16 TITUS ACTED AS GO-BETWEEN WHEN RELATIONS BETWEEN PAUL AND THE CORINTHIANS WERE AT AN ALL-TIME LOW.

HELP!

IT LOOKS LIKE PAUL WROTE AFTER HEARING A CRY FOR HELP FROM TITUS. IT SEEMS THAT THE CHRISTIANS ON CRETE WEREN'T TAKING TITUS SERIOUSLY AS THEIR LEADER. SO PAUL WROTE TO BACK UP FULLY WHAT TITUS WAS SAYING WITH HIS OWN APOSTOLIC AUTHORITY. PAUL USES STRONG LANGUAGE TO PUT THE CRETANS RIGHT. TITUS IS TO 'SHARPLY REBUKE', 'INSTRUCT', 'URGE' AND 'WARN' HIS HEARERS, USING HIS FULL AUTHORITY IN TEACHING THEM. THE LETTER WAS CLEARLY MEANT NOT FOR TITUS' EYES ONLY. IT MUST HAVE STRENGTHENED HIS HAND A LOT IN A HOT SITUATION. AND THE LETTER STILL HAS A LOT TO SAY TO CHURCH LEADERS TODAY.

Phoenix   Heracleon
Lasea

CRETE: NO HOLIDAY FOR TITUS

141

PAUL

Whatever happened to the Apostle Paul?

I don't know. His story seems to end at Acts 28.

THE BOOK OF ACTS TELLS US THAT PAUL WAS ARRESTED BY THE ROMAN AUTHORITIES IN JERUSALEM AFTER A RIOT (ACTS 21). HE APPEALED TO BE TRIED BY THE ROMAN EMPEROR AND WAS SENT BY SHIP TO ROME. HE HAD A BAD VOYAGE (ACTS 27) BUT EVENTUALLY ARRIVED. ACTS CLOSES WITH PAUL UNDER HOUSE ARREST IN ROME. HE LIVED THERE FOR TWO YEARS IN RENTED ACCOMMODATION WAITING FOR HIS TRIAL BEFORE THE EMPEROR. BUT THEN WHAT?

PAUL'S FINAL THREE LETTERS GIVE US SOME SCRAPS OF INFORMATION ABOUT WHAT PAUL DID NEXT...

ACTS 28
PAUL IS UNDER HOUSE ARREST IN ROME

PAUL IS PROBABLY TRIED AND RELEASED, AD 63.

1 TIMOTHY + TITUS
PAUL IS OUT OF PRISON, HAS TRAVELLED TO EPHESUS, NORTHERN GREECE AND CRETE

2 TIMOTHY
PAUL IS BACK IN PRISON IN ROME AGAIN. THE END SEEMS NEAR.

FOR A LONG TIME PAUL HAD WANTED TO VISIT SPAIN TO PREACH THE GOOD NEWS. HE HAD WRITTEN TO THE CHURCH IN ROME...

I would like to see you on my way to Spain, and be helped by you to go there...

ROMANS 15:24

ACCORDING TO SEVERAL EARLY WRITERS, PAUL FULFILLED THIS AMBITION AFTER HIS RELEASE IN AD 63.

The End

IN AD 64, A TERRIBLE FIRE DESTROYED MOST OF ROME. THE EMPEROR NERO WAS BLAMED AND HE NEEDED SOME SCAPEGOATS – FAST. HE CHOSE THE CHRISTIANS AS THEY WERE UNPOPULAR, AND HAD THEM PUT TO DEATH IN THE MOST CRUEL WAYS. IT'S GENERALLY AGREED THAT PAUL WAS A VICTIM OF THIS PERSECUTION, PUT TO DEATH BY A SWORD AROUND THE YEAR AD 67.

Philemon

THIS SHORT, PERSONAL LETTER, WRITTEN BY PAUL, IS ABOUT A SLAVE CALLED 'USEFUL'. THAT'S EXACTLY WHAT HIS MASTER CALLED HIM (<u>ONESIMUS</u> IS THE GREEK WORD FOR 'USEFUL'). BUT THIS NAME WAS A BIT OF A JOKE AS USEFUL WAS ACTUALLY A PRETTY USELESS SLAVE (SEE VERSE 11). HE ENDED UP STEALING FROM HIS MASTER AND THEN RUNNING AWAY. THE PUNISHMENT FOR SLAVES WHO DID THIS SORT OF THING WAS <u>EXTREMELY</u> SEVERE.

USEFUL! Bring in that bottle of wine I gave you!

CRASH!!

That's another bottle of the Sicilian 22 BC gone...

BUT THEN USEFUL MET PAUL. HE BECAME A CHRISTIAN. AND AT LAST HIS LIFE STARTED TO MATCH UP TO HIS SLAVE-NAME AS HE BECAME A MUCH-VALUED COMPANION TO PAUL IN PRISON. HE CONFESSED THAT HE WAS A RUNAWAY SLAVE, AND IT TURNED OUT THAT HIS MASTER, PHILEMON, WAS AN OLD CHRISTIAN FRIEND OF PAUL'S.

To Philemon, Church at Colossae, Asia

SO PAUL SENT USEFUL BACK TO PHILEMON, CARRYING THIS LETTER. HE BEGGED HIM, IN A TACTFUL AND HUMOROUS WAY, TO —

WELL, YOU CAN READ THAT FOR YOURSELF!

SLAVERY

MANY CHURCHES OF THAT TIME CONTAINED SLAVES AND MASTERS. SO WHAT DID PAUL THINK OF SLAVERY?

- HE TOLD SLAVES TO BE GOOD AT IT! BUT IF THEY COULD GAIN THEIR FREEDOM, THEY SHOULD DO SO.
- HE TOLD MASTERS TO TREAT SLAVES WITH HUMANITY.
- HE DIDN'T ACTIVELY WORK FOR ABOLITION — THIS HAD TO COME LATER IN THE CHURCH'S HISTORY.
- HE SAW SLAVERY AS ONE OF THE THINGS CHRIST HAD COME TO DESTROY (SEE GALATIANS 3:28).

HEBREWS

I don't know what to make of this book! I can't even get beyond verse 4!

MOST PEOPLE WHO START TO READ THE LETTER TO THE HEBREWS FIND THAT IT'S SOMETHING OF A FOREIGN BOOK. THAT'S NOT SURPRISING SINCE IT WAS WRITTEN TO A PARTICULAR GROUP OF PEOPLE WITH SPECIAL PROBLEMS. BUT THE MESSAGE OF HEBREWS IS AMAZINGLY RICH, SO IT'S WORTH FINDING OUT WHAT THE WRITER WAS AIMING TO DO.

HE BREWS

SHE BREWS

NON-SEXIST EDITION

Okay. So who was it written for?

HEBREWS WAS MOST LIKELY WRITTEN TO A GROUP OF JEWISH CHRISTIANS. SOME PEOPLE HAVE SUGGESTED THAT THEY WERE THE PRIESTS FROM THE JERUSALEM TEMPLE WHO WERE CONVERTED EARLY ON IN THE BOOK OF ACTS. [HERE THEY ARE...] WHOEVER THEY WERE, THEY HAD BEEN SUFFERING SEVERE OPPOSITION FOR THEIR NEW FAITH. THEY WERE TEMPTED TO GIVE IT ALL UP AND RETURN TO JUDAISM.

The number of disciples in Jerusalem grew larger and larger, and a great number of priests accepted the faith.

ACTS 6:7

Hmmm...

All this persecution gives me a headache! Why don't we just go back to our old faith — after all, it's the same God...

HEBREWS ANSWERS THIS BY SAYING THAT GOING BACK TO A JEWISH FAITH IS NO OPTION FOR CHRISTIANS. JESUS ISN'T JUST AN ALTERNATIVE TO OLD TESTAMENT FAITH, HE IS IN EVERY WAY SUPERIOR TO IT...

144

Just a minute! Can you explain that so that even _I_ can understand what you're saying?

THE WRITER OF HEBREWS SHOWS HOW JESUS IS GREATER THAN THE MOST HIGHLY-VALUED ASPECTS OF THE JEWISH FAITH OF THE OLD TESTAMENT...

ANGELS

In the Jewish religion, angels were important messengers sent by God. But Jesus was greater. He was God's Son. His message is also more important.

HEBREWS 1-2

MOSES

Moses was a central figure to Judaism – he was given the Law by God on Mt Sinai. But Moses was still only a faithful _servant_. Jesus was God's _Son_.

HEBREWS 3:1-6

HIGH PRIEST

The Jewish High Priest offered animal sacrifices to pay for the sins of the people. But Jesus was the perfect High Priest because he never committed any sin himself.

HEBREWS 4:14-7:28

SACRIFICES

The Jewish faith relied on an elaborate system of worship in which animals were regularly sacrificed to pay for human sin. Jesus' death was the perfect sacrifice because of who he was, and because he only had to make _one_ sacrifice.

HEBREWS 9:11-28

SINAI AGREEMENT

This agreement between God and Israel (the 'Old Testament') was the foundation of the Jewish faith. But it was temporary. Jesus' death has brought the new agreement ('New Testament') which is permanent.

HEBREWS 12:18-2A

Is that it?

No! THE WRITER PRESSES HIS POINT HOME WITH A SERIES OF WARNINGS AND ENCOURAGEMENTS:

▷ WARNINGS IN PASSAGES LIKE HEBREWS 6:4-6, HE SAYS THAT TO RENOUNCE THE CHRISTIAN FAITH WOULD BE IRREVERSIBLE.

▷ ENCOURAGEMENTS HEBREWS 11+12 ARE TWO OUTSTANDING CHAPTERS OF THE WHOLE BIBLE. CHAPTER 11 SUMS UP THE TOUGH FAITH OF GOD'S PEOPLE IN THE PAST, AND 12 CALLS US TO FOLLOW THIS EXAMPLE.

JAMES

THIS LETTER WAS WRITTEN BY JAMES.

James who?

WELL, THERE'S BEEN SOME DISAGREEMENT ABOUT THIS. BUT THE TRADITIONAL VIEW IS THAT IT WAS JAMES, THE YOUNGER BROTHER OF JESUS. DURING JESUS' LIFE, HE HAD THOUGHT JESUS WAS A RELIGIOUS NUT. BUT JESUS APPEARED TO HIM ALIVE AGAIN AFTER THE RESURRECTION, AND JAMES BECAME A BELIEVER. HE WENT ON TO LEAD THE CHURCH IN JERUSALEM.

THE HEART OF JAMES' BOOK IS THE CONNECTION BETWEEN FAITH AND ACTION (JAMES 2:14-26). SOME PEOPLE WERE DIVORCING FAITH FROM ACTIONS. THEY SAID —

What's important is what I believe inside. As long as I believe the right things, I can behave exactly as I want!

JAMES ATTACKED THIS — QUITE SAVAGELY. HE SAID TRUE FAITH ALWAYS SHOWS ITSELF IN THE WAY WE BEHAVE. HE GIVES AN EXAMPLE: WHAT GOOD IS IT TO SAY...

God bless you — eat well!

IF YOU DON'T GIVE A HUNGRY PERSON SOMETHING TO EAT?

SO, SAYS JAMES, FAITH AND ACTION SHOULDN'T BE DIVORCED — THEY NATURALLY WORK TOGETHER. HE SUMS IT UP BY SAYING:

66 Faith without works is dead. 99
JAMES 2:17

James then goes on to show how this 'active faith' works out in some very practical situations...

Prejudice against the poor (James 2:1-13

Controlling the tongue (James 3:1-12)

The danger of riches (James 5:1-6)

1 Peter

THIS LETTER WAS WRITTEN FOR A VERY PRACTICAL REASON. IT WAS MEANT TO HELP CHRISTIANS PREPARE THEMSELVES FOR PERSECUTION BY THE ROMAN STATE. IT IS ONE OF THE BEST-LOVED NEW TESTAMENT LETTERS, BECAUSE OF ITS WARMTH AND AFFECTION FOR ITS READERS.

PETER, ONE OF JESUS' FIRST DISCIPLES, WROTE THE LETTER FROM ROME. AND AS HE WROTE, THE CHRISTIANS IN ROME WERE SUFFERING THE FIRST WAVE OF VIOLENT PERSECUTION UNDER THE SADISTIC EMPEROR, NERO.

> But how did _that_ happen? I thought the Romans were fairly tolerant of Christians...

THEY HAD BEEN — UNTIL NOW. ON 19 JULY AD 64, THE GREAT FIRE OF ROME BROKE OUT. THE ANGRY CROWDS HELD NERO RESPONSIBLE FOR STARTING THE FIRE. SO HE POINTED THE FINGER AT THE INNOCENT ROMAN CHRISTIANS. THEY DID IT, HE SAID.

THIS WAY

TACITUS, THE ROMAN HISTORIAN, DETAILS THE CRUEL PERSECUTION...

> They were clad in the hides of beasts and torn to death by dogs; others were crucified, others set on fire to serve to illuminate the night when daylight failed.

ANNALS 15:44

THIS PERSECUTION HAPPENED ONLY IN ROME. BUT IT WAS NEWS ALL OVER THE EMPIRE. FROM NOW ON, CHRISTIANS WERE FAIR GAME.

PETER'S LETTER WAS WRITTEN TO CHRISTIANS IN WHAT IS NOW TURKEY. IT'S A KIND OF MANUAL TO ENABLE CHRISTIANS TO SURVIVE PERSECUTION WITH THEIR FAITH COMPLETELY INTACT. THE LETTER IS FULL OF JOY, AND IN IT PETER MAKES THE FOLLOWING POINTS...

HOW TO FACE PERSECUTION (AND STILL BELIEVE IN GOD) BY PETER

▷ CHRISTIANS HAVE A LIVING HOPE. THE NEW LIFE OF JESUS GIVES THEM STRENGTH NOW, AND HIS SECOND COMING GIVES THEM HOPE FOR THE FUTURE.

▷ CHRISTIANS SUFFER IN THE SAME WAY THAT JESUS DID — HE IS THEIR EXAMPLE.

▷ CHRISTIANS ARE CALLED TO LIVE DIFFERENTLY FROM THE WAY THE REST OF THE WORLD LIVES.

2 PETER

Who wrote this one?

Oh dear! I wish you hadn't asked that!

IT'S UNLIKELY THAT IT WAS PETER, DISCIPLE OF JESUS. THIS LETTER IS COMPLETELY DIFFERENT IN STYLE, CONTENT AND CHARACTER FROM 1 PETER. AND IT TOOK LONGER FOR THE CHURCH TO ACCEPT THIS BOOK INTO THE NEW TESTAMENT THAN ANY OTHER — SOMETHING THAT WOULDN'T HAVE HAPPENED TO A GENUINE PETER LETTER.

But the very first verse says: 'From Simon Peter...' Are you saying that's a lie?

NO. IT SOUNDS STRANGE NOW, BUT IT WAS QUITE COMMON IN THOSE DAYS FOR UNKNOWN WRITERS TO WRITE UNDER THE NAME OF A FAMOUS AUTHOR THEY ADMIRED. IN THIS CASE, THE WRITER MAY HAVE WANTED TO PUT THE MESSAGE GOD HAD GIVEN HIM IN PETER'S NAME, BECAUSE HE FELT UNWORTHY TO SPEAK FOR HIMSELF. THERE WAS NOTHING WRONG IN DOING THIS.

---

2 PETER IS LIKE A LOADED GUN. IN ITS SIGHTS IS A GROUP OF PERSUASIVE MEN WHO WERE TEACHING DANGEROUS IDEAS.

THEY SAID...

Now that we're Christians, we are free! We can do whatever we want. Money, women, fame - the lot!

Don't worry about this teaching that Jesus will come back again. It hasn't happened yet, and never will! Life goes on the same.

2 PETER ANSWERED...

These people aren't free - they're slaves to habits that'll destroy them. And they bring the Christian faith into disrepute.

Jesus hasn't yet returned because God is patient. He holds back to give people time to turn to him. But he will come.

1, 2 + 3 John

THESE THREE LETTERS WERE PROBABLY THE LAST OF ALL THE NEW TESTAMENT WRITINGS TO BE PUT DOWN ON PAPER. THE WRITER WAS PROBABLY JOHN, WHO ALSO WROTE JOHN'S GOSPEL.

1 JOHN
To: Everyone

2 JOHN
To: The Dear Lady + her children

3 JOHN
To: Gaius, church leader

1 JOHN READS MORE LIKE A TRACT THAN A LETTER. IT ENCOURAGES CHRISTIANS TO LOVE GOD AND EACH OTHER, AND IT WARNS AGAINST ENEMIES OF THE FAITH. 2 JOHN IS A REAL LETTER, WRITTEN WITH THE SAME AIMS AS 1 JOHN. IT IS ADDRESSED TO 'THE DEAR LADY' (A LOCAL CHURCH), 'AND HER CHILDREN' (ITS MEMBERS).

3 JOHN IS A PERSONAL NOTE TO A CHURCH LEADER, GAIUS. IT ENCOURAGES HIM AND WARNS AGAINST A RATHER PROUD LEADER IN A NEARBY CHURCH.

SO WHAT WERE THESE ENEMIES OF THE FAITH SAYING?

Listen! I've got some <u>secret</u> teaching to give you which is much better than what you've been taught before. Everything physical is completely evil. The world is evil and so are our bodies. So Jesus wasn't really human — God couldn't get involved in such an evil world. And since our bodies are evil anyway, it doesn't matter what we do with them. We can behave as we like!

JOHN ANSWERED THIS BY SAYING...

☐ JESUS WAS A TRUE, FLESH-AND-BLOOD HUMAN BEING. JOHN HAD HEARD, SEEN AND TOUCHED HIM (1 JOHN 1:1). AND SO THE PHYSICAL SIDE OF LIFE ISN'T IN ITSELF EVIL.

☐ IT IS IMPORTANT HOW WE LIVE OUR LIVES. WE MUST LIVE AS GOD WANTS, BECAUSE 'GOD IS LIGHT' (1 JOHN 1:5).

☐ WE MUST ALSO LOVE EACH OTHER, BECAUSE 'GOD IS LOVE' (1 JOHN 4:8). IT'S NO GOOD SAYING YOU LOVE GOD IF YOU HATE OTHER PEOPLE. SO BEING A CHRISTIAN, ACCORDING TO JOHN, IS A PRACTICAL, DOWN-TO-EARTH BUSINESS.

Jude

LIKE SO MANY OF THE NEW TESTAMENT LETTERS, JUDE WAS WRITTEN TO ATTACK FALSE TEACHERS WHO HAD INFILTRATED THE CHURCH. (IRONICALLY, HERESY HAS OFTEN BEEN VALUABLE TO THE CHRISTIAN FAITH, BECAUSE IT MADE JUDE, PAUL AND THE OTHERS SPELL OUT <u>EXACTLY</u> WHAT THE TRUTH IS. THIS SHOWS HOW EVIL CAN OFTEN SELF-DESTRUCT!)

So who was this Jude?

TRADITIONALLY, HE'S BEEN IDENTIFIED AS A YOUNGER BROTHER OF JESUS. HE CALLS HIMSELF JAMES' BROTHER, AND JESUS HAD TWO BROTHERS OF THOSE NAMES (MARK 6:3).

JUDE TELLS US THAT HE WAS IN THE MIDDLE OF WRITING A LONGER, MORE DETAILED LETTER SETTING OUT THE CHRISTIAN FAITH, WHEN BAD NEWS ARRIVED. THE FALSE TEACHERS WERE AT IT AGAIN...

Hold it! This is urgent!

SO JUDE PUT HIS LONGER LETTER ASIDE (PERHAPS HE NEVER GOT BACK TO IT!) AND WROTE INSTEAD A RED-HOT DENUNCIATION OF THESE EVIL TEACHERS.

JUDE IS PERHAPS BEST KNOWN FOR THE TREMENDOUS PRAYER THAT CLOSES HIS BOOK. IT'S APPROPRIATE TOO THAT THIS PRAYER ADDS THE FINISHING TOUCH TO THE SECTION OF NEW TESTAMENT LETTERS...

To him who is able to keep you from falling and to present you before his glorious presence without fault and with great joy — to the only God our Saviour be glory, majesty, power and authority, through Jesus Christ our Lord, before all ages, now and for evermore!

JUDE 24-25

IT'S A PRAYER FULL OF CONFIDENCE THAT GOD WILL ACHIEVE WHAT HE SET OUT TO DO — DESPITE THE STRATAGEMS OF EVIL. AND IT'S A PRAYER TO WHICH PAUL, JAMES, PETER, JOHN AND THE OTHER LETTER-WRITERS WOULD HAVE SAID —

Amen!

THE APOCALYPSE

THIS SECTION CONTAINS THE BOOK OF REVELATION

AND THAT'S ALL, FOLKS!

Revelation

THE BOOK OF REVELATION IS ALSO KNOWN AS THE APOCALYPSE. THIS GREEK WORD MEANS TO 'UNCOVER' OR TO REVEAL WHAT WAS HIDDEN. THE BOOK WAS WRITTEN BY A CHRISTIAN CALLED JOHN ON THE GREEK ISLAND OF PATMOS.

UNFORTUNATELY NOT. JOHN HAD BEEN SENT IN EXILE TO PATMOS AS A PUNISHMENT FOR PREACHING THE GOOD NEWS. CHRISTIANS AROUND THE ROMAN EMPIRE WERE BEING PERSECUTED AT THAT TIME, WHICH IS WHY THE BOOK WAS WRITTEN.

Oh! So he was on vacation then?

THE PERSECUTION THAT PROBABLY FORMED THE BACKGROUND FOR JOHN'S APOCALYPSE WAS STARTED BY THE EMPEROR DOMITIAN, WHO RULED FROM AD 81 TO 96. HE BEGAN TO CALL HIMSELF 'MASTER AND GOD' AND DEMANDED THAT PEOPLE SHOULD WORSHIP HIM. THOSE WHO REFUSED TO DO SO WERE SEEN AS 'TRAITORS' AND COULD BE PUT TO DEATH. MANY CHRISTIANS SUFFERED AND DIED FOR THEIR FAITH AT THIS TIME.

Bow down, worms!

DOMITIAN

ALL OF THIS LED CHRISTIANS TO ASK QUESTIONS LIKE THESE:

Why is evil triumphing over good?

Will all Christians be wiped out?

How long will it be before God does something?

JOHN'S APOCALYPSE WAS A DIRECT RESPONSE TO THE CONFUSION, DOUBT AND DESPAIR OF MANY CHRISTIANS. IT CAME TO HIM IN A SERIES OF BIZARRE VISIONS, WHICH ARE IN THE SAME 'FAMILY' AS THE VISIONS IN THE OLD TESTAMENT BOOKS OF DANIEL AND ZECHARIAH.

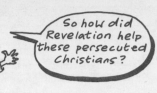

So how did Revelation help these persecuted Christians?

AT THE HEART OF JOHN'S VISIONS IS A VIVID PICTURE OF THE GOD WHO RULES OVER ALL HISTORY. THERE IS A MIGHTY CLASH BETWEEN THE FORCES OF GOOD AND EVIL, BUT THE VICTORY OF GOD OVER THE DEVIL IS NEVER REALLY IN DOUBT. CHRISTIANS WERE REMINDED THAT THE POWER OF ROME, WHICH WAS BENT AGAINST THEM, WAS PATHETICALLY WEAK UNDER GOD'S POWERFUL HAND.

Meet the Cast

THIS LIST OF THE CHARACTERS IN REVELATION GIVES AN IDEA OF WHAT JOHN'S VISIONS ARE LIKE, AND HELP IN FINDING YOUR WAY AROUND...

☐ THE LAMB (REVELATION 5, 14 + 19) SYMBOLIZES JESUS WHO GAVE UP HIS LIFE AS A SACRIFICE.

☐ THE FOUR HORSE RIDERS (REVELATION 6) AREN'T ON A QUIET SUNDAY AFTERNOON RIDE. THEY BRING CONQUEST, WAR, FAMINE AND DEATH.

☐ SEVEN ANGELS WITH SEVEN TRUMPETS (REVELATION 8-11). EACH TRUMPET-BLAST HERALDS GOD'S JUDGMENT.

☐ THE WOMAN GIVING BIRTH (REVELATION 12) REPRESENTS GOD'S PEOPLE. HER CHILD IS THE MESSIAH.

☐ THE DRAGON (REVELATION 12 + 20) HAS SEVEN HEADS AND TEN HORNS. THIS IS SATAN.

☐ THE TWO BEASTS (REVELATION 13) SYMBOLIZE ANTI-GOD POWERS.

☐ SEVEN ANGELS WITH SEVEN PLAGUES (REVELATION 15-16), LIKE THE EXODUS PLAGUES.

☐ THE PROSTITUTE OF BABYLON (REVELATION 17-18) SYMBOLIZED THE CITY OF ROME. BUT EVERY ERA HAS ITS OWN 'BABYLON'.

☐ THE BRIDE (REVELATION 19) IS THE OPPOSITE OF THE PROSTITUTE. SHE REPRESENTS THE CHURCH.

☐ THE RIDER OF THE WHITE HORSE (REVELATION 19) IS THE SON OF GOD IN HIS GREAT POWER.

THE BOOK CLOSES IN CHAPTERS 21 AND 22 WITH A VISION OF A NEW HEAVEN AND EARTH. THEY STUNNINGLY DESCRIBE THE COMPLETION OF GOD'S WORK IN JESUS, WITH THE RE-CREATION OF A WORLD THAT WAS SPOILED BY HUMAN SIN. IT'S APPROPRIATE THAT THE BIBLE ENDS IN THIS WAY: STARTING IN THE GARDEN OF EDEN, ENDING IN THE CITY OF GOD.

7 Churches

JOHN ADDRESSED THE BOOK
OF REVELATION TO SEVEN
CHURCHES IN THE ROMAN
PROVINCE OF ASIA (TODAY'S
WESTERN TURKEY). THE FIRST
THREE CHAPTERS OF THE BOOK
CONSIST OF A SERIES OF
NOTES ADDRESSED TO EACH
CHURCH.

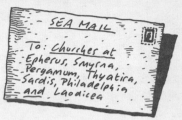

SEA MAIL

To: Churches at
Ephesus, Smyrna,
Pergamum, Thyatira,
Sardis, Philadelphia
and Laodicea

JOHN HAS
A SPECIAL
MESSAGE
FROM GOD
FOR ALL
SEVEN
CHURCHES.
EACH LETTER
HAS THE
SAME
STRUCTURE...

To Church 'x'

P.T.O.

Opening
The message is from the
heavenly person John saw
in Revelation 1: 9-20.

Middle
Encouragements and
warnings are given. Each
church gets a different
mixture!

Ending
A promise: 'To those who
win the victory I will give...'
The reward promised
echoes the descriptions of
the new heaven and earth
at the end of Revelation.

So what's
in these
letters?

THE SEVEN CHURCHES, TOWARDS
THE END OF THE FIRST
CENTURY AD, WERE FACING
MANY DIFFERENT PROBLEMS:
FALSE APOSTLES, STRANGE
TEACHING, PAGAN RELIGIONS, EMPEROR
WORSHIP, PERSECUTION, ETC. BUT EVEN
WORSE WERE THE PROBLEMS _INSIDE_ THESE
CHURCHES: COOLING OF LOVE FOR GOD AND
EACH OTHER, SEXUAL IMMORALITY, APATHY,
SELF-SATISFACTION. TWO OF THE CHURCHES
(SMYRNA AND PHILADELPHIA) RECEIVE NO
CRITICISM. BUT THE REST ARE GIVEN SOME
SHARPLY-WORDED WARNINGS.

UNDERSTANDING IT

I'm confused! How am I supposed to understand this Book of Revelation? Is it about the future? Does it give us a date for the end of the world? And how much further have we got to trudge?

Well...

HERE ARE THREE STEPS TO HELP YOU GET STARTED ON THE MESSAGE OF THIS GREAT BOOK...

Start with the past

THIS WAY

START BY LOOKING AT THE BOOK THROUGH THE EYES OF ITS FIRST READERS. THIS IS TRUE FOR ANY PART OF THE BIBLE. SO REMEMBER THAT REVELATION'S FIRST READERS WERE PERSECUTED, LOOKING FOR ENCOURAGEMENT. AND THEY WOULD SEE REFERENCES TO ROME AND ITS HOPED-FOR DESTRUCTION THROUGHOUT THE BOOK.

Go on to the future

THE BOOK OF REVELATION CLAIMS TO BE A PROPHECY ABOUT THE END OF TIME — SO IT'S NOT JUST ABOUT THE FALL OF ANCIENT ROME. GOD'S JUDGMENT ON THE ROMAN EMPIRE IS A PICTURE OF WHAT HE WILL DO TO <u>ALL</u> EVIL POWERS AT THE END OF TIME. SO THERE ARE TWO LEVELS OF PROPHECY AT WORK HERE. ONE IS ABOUT THE FALL OF ROME. AND THE SECOND IS ABOUT THE FALL OF THE EVIL THAT INSPIRED ROME. REVELATION GIVES US A SHOCKING PICTURE OF THE DEVIOUSNESS AND POWER OF EVIL, AND HOW GOD WILL OBLITERATE IT FOR EVER.

Don't trip up over details

SOME PEOPLE HAVE TRIED TO FIND MODERN MEANINGS FOR ALL THE TINIEST DETAILS IN THE BOOK. OTHERS TRY TO WORK OUT A TIMETABLE OF EVENTS FROM IT. AVOID THIS SORT OF THING LIKE THE PLAGUE! REVELATION <u>ISN'T</u> A CODE BOOK, WAITING TO BE CRACKED. THE WRITING IS POETIC, AND THE DETAILS ARE THERE TO BUILD UP AN INSPIRING OVERALL PICTURE OF GOD DEFEATING EVIL.

THE END

BIBLE MAPBOOK

SIMON JENKINS

This book of cartoon-style maps brings to life the significant events of the Bible. It has been designed for those of us who are foreigners to the Bible's world, and who wouldn't know whether to turn left or right to reach Bethlehem. It gives a guided tour to the famous faces and happenings of the Old and New Testaments.

The *Bible Mapbook* has the following features:
- 3-D computer graphics put you right in the heart of the action, the heat of the battle . . .
- Maps follow the same order of events as the Bible
- One map per event makes it easy to follow the action
- Concise notes give rapid access to essential information
- Covers the whole sweep of Bible history

'A delightfully idiot-proof guide which puts people and places where they belong with a minimum of fuss.'
Family

'Charts the names, places, journeys and battles of the Bible. A helpful aid.'
Eternity

'This bird's-eye view of biblical history is bound to be a winner.'
Methodist Recorder

0 85648 887 9